THE
WORLD
OF
ARMAND
HAMMER

The Hammers, Red Square, March 1982.

With Vice Chairman Deng Xiaoping, Beijing,
Great Hall of the People, April 1984.

Aboard Oxy One, 37,000 feet over
North Dakota, February 1982.

February 1982: Honorary
citizenship in Vinci, Italy, birthplace
of Leonardo da Vinci.

Opening day, Los Angeles Olympics, 28 July 1984.

With Dr. Jonas Salk, La Jolla, California, 1982.

THE
WORLD
OF
ARMAND
HAM

MER

Text and
Photographs
by
John Bryson

Introduction by Walter Cronkite   Designed by Will Hopkins and Ira Friedlander
Harry N. Abrams, Inc., Publishers, New York

Dedicated
to Nancy Guild Bryson,
who makes everything possible

Art Directors:
Will Hopkins
Ira Friedlander

Art Assistants:
Miriam Weinberg
Reyhan Bray
Joseph Baron
Ronna Gilbert

Text Editors:
Stephen Brewer
Mary Beth Brewer

ISBN 0–8109–1093–4

Printed and bound in Japan

4 A.M., 26 April 1984: Refueling stop, Novosibirsk, Siberia; Dr. Hammer peruses Izvestia.

Introduction by Walter Cronkite	19
The Plane	20
The Doctor's Office	32
Early Days	38
Home: Los Angeles	54
The Codex Goes to Italy	70
Movers & Shakers	80
The Royal Family	90
Russia	94
Home: Moscow	126
Arabian Horses	130
The Beautiful People	140
Good Works	152
A Hunt in Hungary	174
Washington Elite	182
An Empire of Art	190
Home: New York	204
Occidental Petroleum	208
China	226
The World in a Week	244

INTRODUCTION

With that felicity of phrase for which he won his justified fame, the late Bob Considine in his biography of Armand Hammer at one point referred to him as, at seventy-five, "still possessed of his marbles and his beans."

A decade has passed since Bob wrote those lines, and so has Bob. But not Armand Hammer. And it is possible now to identify the beans of which he was still possessed at seventy-five and of which he still has an abundance today. They are jumping beans.

This incredible man seems perpetually on the move. To say that he commutes to corners of the world that the less-traveled would call "remote" or even "exotic" is to understate the case. Commuting suggests something plebian, everyday, ordinary—the train ride back and forth from suburbia or, in the case of today's international business, entertainment, or social jet set, the supersonic Concorde or perhaps a private executive jet.

That isn't the way Armand Hammer does it. He doesn't really commute anywhere—from his Los Angeles headquarters to Moscow or New York or Beijing or Lima. When he goes to all those places and a few score other capitals and commercial and cultural centers he simply moves the comforts of headquarters and home with him. He travels by a private Boeing 727 with his own bedroom and office and some staff space occupying the huge interior that in its passenger liner configuration would hold 132 people.

This is a far cry from his first overseas trip. He was barely twenty-three then. He was born in New York's lower East Side, son of a Russian Jewish immigrant doctor, turned socialist and Unitarian. He was a concert-grade pianist, an honor graduate of Columbia medical school, and already had become a millionaire in the pharmaceutical business he built up while still a student. (And that, as any old timer will tell you, was when the dollar was worth something. A million then is worth around six million today!)

His intentions were philanthropic on that first voyage soon after the Columbia graduation, in 1921. He hoped to use his new medical knowledge to help relieve the disease and starvation that had beset Russia in the wake of World War I and its Communist revolution. Never did anyone work harder to give something away. He was jailed by the suspicious British trying to isolate the Russian Red Plague; the Germans looked on him with suspicion, and even the Russian representatives in Berlin, xenophobic then as now, held up his visa.

Hacking his way through the bureaucratic red tape was only part of the exercise. In contrast to his own magic carpet that now whisks him to Moscow, on that first trip he huddled in a vermin-infested railway coach, lighted only by the candle he had thought to bring along. In Moscow he lived for weeks in a filthy room while trying to beat down the doors of intransigent bureaucrats.

Even the indomitable Hammer was about to give up and return home when, on a sponsored trip to the Urals, he was struck by the mineral riches of the region, uselessly stockpiled, while the starving population beat against the sides of the railway coach begging for a crust of bread.

He ordered his associates in the United States to ship immediately a million bushels of grain to Russia. He hoped he could recover at least some of the cost by trading it for some of the Urals' riches. Lenin heard of his audacity, ordered him to Moscow and ended up giving him a concession to bring American industry and goods to the Soviets. The rest, as they say, is history.

Hammer never got around to practising medicine. Instead he became one of the world's leading industrialists, one of its great art collectors, an outstandingly successful cattle breeder, an incredibly generous philanthropist, an almost unique bridge between communism and capitalism, and the confidante of presidents, prime ministers, sheiks, shahs, emirs, and monarchs of numerous and assorted varieties. His business conquests have not been without controversy but, unless he is a superb actor along with his other talents, he clearly enjoys the fray.

It is too bad that he did not think, in 1921, of taking a photographer along on that first significant, even historic, Russian trip. But that idea did come to him later, and here is photographer John Bryson's fascinating, engrossing documentation of the truly incredible world of Armand Hammer.

Walter Cronkite

At Claridge's Hotel, his London lodgings for sixty-two years, Hammer is greeted by the cockaded doorman as the purring Rolls awaits.

THE PLANE

The engines are already running on the white Boeing 727 as it sits waiting on a ramp at the edge of the Los Angeles airport. Precisely on schedule, the long black limousine sweeps through the gate, circles *Oxy One*, and stops at the back stairs. Dr. Armand Hammer climbs aboard, the stairs snap closed, and the plane taxis to the runway; within minutes it is climbing over the blue Pacific Ocean.

His bulging briefcase is waiting in his office. He enters his spacious bedroom and puts on his traveling sweater and slippers before settling down to work. Before long, he will pick up his telephone and begin placing calls around the world.

Oxy One is a special plane. Purchased in July 1980, it is a traveling command post for the eighty-seven-year-old tycoon, who travels between continents like most people go back and forth to the corner store. The plane is fitted with extra fuel tanks, which give it a range of more than 4,000 nautical miles. With the plane's sophisticated communications system, the Doctor can make telephone calls anywhere on earth, and a satellite telex takes over when there are problems with telephone ground stations.

In 1984 Hammer was airborne for the equivalent of twenty-four days. He flew 271,944 nautical miles, including four trips to the Soviet Union, thirteen trips to England, two trips to France, and visits to China, Canada, Yugoslavia, Italy, Switzerland, Hungary, Israel, Austria, Colombia, Peru, Bermuda, Spain, Jamaica, Mexico, the Azores, and Venezuela. He also made eighteen trips to Washington, sixteen to New York, and visits to a score of American cities—all the while conducting business from his airborne command post.

To relax between stops, he and Mrs. Hammer, holding hands, watch old Charlie Chaplin movies on one of the plane's two TV sets.

The fruit bowl on board is always filled. Oxy One's clock shows local time, destination time, and how many hours to get there.

In his airborne bedroom, the Doctor relaxes and makes a phone call. In 1984, he was in the air 584.4 hours.

Above, left. Hammer in Zurich with
Fred Gross, his pilot. Gross, who was a
pilot at a small airfield near Hammer's
New Jersey farm, began flying Hammer's
Beechcraft in 1950 and since then has
logged 12,000 hours with the Doctor. He
flew Hammer's personal Boeing 727,
Oxy One, 271,944 nautical miles in
1984. Gross also commands the
Occidental fleet of nineteen planes.

Above. Relaxing on a solitary flight across the country, Hammer has tea and watches one of his favorite Charlie Chaplin movies; the plane library has practically every known Chaplin film. Left. Late at night, flying over the North Pole, Hammer confers with producer Jerry Weintraub about cultural negotiations with the Soviet Union and China.

When Oxy One flies into the Soviet Union, the Russians send a pilot and navigator to pick up the plane at London's Heathrow Airport; they do not fly the plane but sit in the cockpit for the trip to and from Moscow. Hammer is the only person in the world who regularly flies his private plane into the Soviet Union and China.

It is forty below and the arctic winds are blowing at twenty-five knots as Oxy One is fueled at the ice-locked airport at Goose Bay, Canada, for the polar flight to Europe. The door opens and a mink-coated figure descends the stairs. Dr. Hammer is going to the terminal to make a phone call.

The Hammers arrive at Moscow's Sheremetyevo Airport, where they are escorted to the V.I.P. lounge while their luggage is whisked through customs and their passports are quickly stamped.

THE DOCTOR'S OFFICE

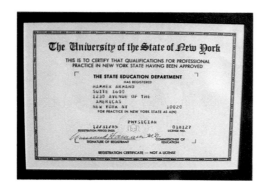

Above, top. At the telephone console next to Hammer's desk, eight clocks show the hour in various world capitals, so he will know the time wherever he is calling. Above. Hammer keeps his New York doctor's license current, though he has not practiced medicine since graduating from Columbia medical school in June 1921.

Hammer runs the Occidental empire from a small pocket calendar book where he records all of his forthcoming trips and meetings. His office is filled with mementos, awards, medals, antique clocks, and letters from American Presidents. He sits beneath a Rubens painting as he telephones around the world. In another corner is a new painting of Chinese horsewomen, *Gaiety in the Grassland.* Chinese leader Deng Xiaoping and Hu Yao Bang, Chairman of the Chinese Communist Party, presented the painting to Hammer during a visit to Beijing in April 1984.

On Hammer's desk are three canceled checks set in plastic, each for $1 billion or more. One is for the largest industrial refinancing to date of an American corporation, the other two are the debt Occidental incurred in the Cities Service acquisition, paid off in only one year.

The battered pocket calendar book that charts the Hammer schedule. This month, March 1985, he has jotted down trips and meetings in such far-flung places as Garden Grove, California, Washington, D.C., Düsseldorf, Moscow, Paris, London, Mallorca, Pakistan, and Oman.

FLOWER: JONQUIL
1985
THURSDAY
FRIDAY
SATUR
1
2
7
8
9
14
15
16
21
22
23
28
29
30
1985 EDITION
©1964-1985 SEE-LINE COMPANY, HOUSTON, PENNSYLVANIA. MADE IN U.S.A.

Above. A brass plaque is from television religious leader Dr. Robert Schuller of the Crystal Cathedral in Garden Grove, California.

Above, right. Three awards: the small oil pumper is a gift from Goldman, Sachs & Co. honoring the Cities Service acquisition; the soaring figures are the Oil Industry Council for the City of Hope's Man of the Year Award; and beside it is an award from the Los Angeles Area Chamber of Commerce for Excellence through Energy.

Right. Lasma Arabians, of Scottsdale, Arizona, presented the Hammers with a dashing statue of a famous Arabian stallion, Bask.

Far right. Models of Oxy One and an oil well depicting Oxy's first oil and gas field at Lathrop, California, in 1961, cluster in a window with photographs of the famous.

Above. *A painting by Rubens,* Venus
Wounded by a Thorn, *is behind
Hammer's desk. Beneath it are
autographed photos of American
Presidents Herbert Hoover, Franklin D.
Roosevelt, Harry Truman, Dwight
Eisenhower, John F. Kennedy, Lyndon
Johnson, Gerald Ford, Jimmy Carter,
and Ronald Reagan, as well as of Lenin,
Pope John Paul II, First Secretary János
Kádár of Hungary, Prime Minister
Margaret Thatcher of Great Britain,
Prime Ministers Shimon Peres and
Yitzhak Shamir of Israel, President Zia
of Pakistan, former General Secretary
Leonid Brezhnev of the Soviet Union,
King Juan Carlos and Queen Sofia of
Spain, President Anwar el-Sadat of
Egypt, and Vice Chairman Deng
Xiaoping of China.*

EARLY DAYS

He rates ninety-six lines in *Who's Who*, where his occupation is given simply as "Armand Hammer, petroleum-company executive, art patron."

Even that accounting of awards, achievements, and decorations does not fully delineate a fraction of Hammer's activities. And should his efforts to find a cure for cancer and to achieve world peace come to fruition, the eighty-seven-year-old entrepreneur will have touched every life on earth.

Armand Hammer was born on New York's Lower East Side on May 21, 1898. His name, like his life and career, is the stuff of legends. Though Hammer is the epitome of capitalism, his physician father was a dedicated member of the Socialist Labor Party, and legend has it that the baby was named after the Party's symbol of an arm and fist holding a hammer. Another widely held story contends that Hammer was named after Arm & Hammer, the famous brand of bicarbonate of soda (years later he tried to buy the company). Hammer says his father, who was educated in France, told him that he was named after the lover, Armand, in Dumas's novel *Camille*.

The Hammers were Jewish immigrants from Russia. Armand's grandfather, Jacob William Hammer, brought his wife and baby son, Julius, to the United States in 1875 and settled in Branford, Connecticut. Julius Hammer was a remarkable man. At the age of fifteen, swinging a sledgehammer as a day laborer in a foundry, he joined a labor union and later became a member of the radical Socialist Labor Party in a period when most Americans regarded socialists as bearded, bomb-throwing anarchists. He moved to New York, seeking opportunity and a chance to make something of himself.

Julius found a job in a small Bowery drugstore, applied himself, and focused his mind on learning the business. He became a registered pharmacist and eventually bought the drugstore from his boss. He soon opened two more ghetto drugstores, brought his older half-brothers to New York to be trained as pharmacists, and put them to work. Appalled at what he considered to be the exorbitant prices charged by national drug firms for standard medicines, he began manufacturing his own pharmaceuticals in a loft on the Upper East Side.

At a socialist outing, Julius met a young widow who had a baby son, Harry, and the couple fell in love. Rose Robinson had been born in Russia and was brought to America as a child. She married the ambitious young pharmacist, and their first child, Armand, was born on the Lower East Side in a cold-water flat above one of Julius's drugstores.

Motivated by his socialist ideal that helping mankind was more important than making money, Julius Hammer decided to become a doctor. Though he had no formal education in the United States, and at twenty-four was considered to be far too old to go back to school, he managed to pass the entrance examinations and was admitted to the Columbia College of Physicians and Surgeons four months after little Armand was born. His drive was prodigious; for four years he ran his drugstores and his pharmaceutical business and attended medical school. He graduated in 1902, sold his businesses, and hung out his shingle as a general practitioner in the Bronx.

"He was a great humanitarian," Armand Hammer says of his father. "He was hard-working, a very decent man. He'd make daily house calls among the poor people of the Bronx, and if a patient didn't have any money, not only did he not send him a bill, he'd leave him some money for medicine."

Though he has been an avowed capitalist since early youth, Armand Hammer understands his hard-working father's motivations, which eventually led him to become a driving force in the formation of the American Communist Party. "As a young man, my father got a job in a steel mill," he says, "and that's where he got his socialist-Marxist background. He came to be sympathetic to the poor and exploited . . . he was imbued with Marxist theories and he felt that communism was the wave of the future. I didn't share my father's views," says Hammer. "I was a capitalist when I was a student in medical school. I made my first million as a student."

By the time young Armand Hammer entered Columbia's medical school in 1917, his father

Young Armand Hammer, age 12, in Meriden, Connecticut, in 1910.

had invested his life savings in another pharmaceutical firm, Allied Drug and Chemical Corporation, which was soon facing bankruptcy because of a dishonest partner. His father asked him to take over the business, but to stay in medical school. "I did it, son," he said, "and you can do it, too."

At nineteen, Armand Hammer was running a full-size business. He gave a classmate room and

Hammer's parents, Rose and Julius, in 1910. Julius pursued the American dream, working his way from steel-mill laborer to medical doctor.

40

board to take voluminous notes that he studied at night. Selling shampoos, medicinal alcohols, and pharmaceutical drugs, the family firm prospered and moved to larger quarters. Soon 1,500 employees were working for the young medical student.

At the same time, Julius was expanding his support of the radical movement and had been named commercial attaché for the newly opened, unofficial Soviet Embassy in New York that was headed by Ludwig Martens, who was later deported.

Prohibition was the law in the United States, and the young Hammer learned that when mixed with ginger ale, tincture of ginger makes a ginger-ale highball with plenty of kick. He cornered the market on ginger, then branched into bonded whiskey to sell under prescription in drugstores.

The young Hammer graduated from medical school with honors in June 1921 and decided to get out of business. "My thoughts were not just on making money," he said later. "I wanted to throw myself into medicine. I was to intern at Bellevue Hospital, and I had about six months to wait, so I decided to sell the business to my employees and devote myself to medicine, particularly to bacteriology. There was a typhus outbreak in Russia, and I thought it would be a good experience for me to go there. I also thought it would please my father."

Hammer's father was now in prison. It was the height of the Red scare that followed World War I, and one of Julius Hammer's patients had died after a therapeutic abortion. He was sent to Sing Sing for three years. Armand Hammer never gave up the fight to clear his father's name. In later years Julius Hammer was pardoned by Governor Al Smith of New York, who wrote that his investigation showed that Hammer had no criminal intent. The New York Board of Regents restored Hammer's license to practice medicine, something it never does for a convicted abortionist.

Armand sold the business for $2 million and bought a World War I army surplus field hospital for $100,000, stocked it with $60,000 worth of supplies, and bought an ambulance for $15,000. When he arrived in Moscow after an excruciating eighty-hour train trip from Riga, Latvia, he found that the Russian capital was devastated from the revolution.

"Moscow was utter desolation," he says in the autobiography he wrote after he left Russia in 1930 (*The Quest of the Romanoff Treasure*; Payson, 1932). "The stores were all empty, their windows broken, or their fronts hidden by boarding. As we neared the center of the town there were more people but little traffic, save for an occasional wagon and a shabby cab. The people seemed clad in rags, hardly any wore stockings or shoes, but had wrappings of dirty cloth around their feet and legs; others wore felt boots; the

Young Dr. Armand Hammer, just before he left for Russia.

children were all barefoot. No one seemed to smile, everyone looked dirty and dejected. . . ."

Years later, the American oil billionaire J. Paul Getty reported that when Hammer was asked the secret of making millions, he replied, "There's nothing to it. You merely wait for a revolution in Russia. Then you pack all your warm clothes and go there. Once you've arrived, you start making the rounds of the government bureaus that are concerned with trade, with buying and selling. There probably won't be more than two or three hundred of them. . . ."

A bureaucrat from the Foreign Office deposited Hammer at the Savoy Hotel in a dingy room

Portrait of Lenin presented to his young friend Hammer; this picture is now in the Doctor's office.

To courade *Armand Hammer* from *M. Oulianoff (Lenin)* 10.XI.1921

В. Ленин

with a bed and mattress, but no sheets or blankets, a grease-stained table, two rickety chairs, a cupboard, and a population of rats and bedbugs. After a few days of discomfort, illness, hunger, and absentee officials, the young doctor began making plans to leave his field hospital to the Russians and depart the chaos of revolution. Though the Commissar of Public Health painted a dismal picture of medical-supply shortages, of patients undergoing operations without anesthetics, and of bandages being sterilized over and over for reuse, Hammer waited in Moscow for the return of the official in charge of assigning foreign doctors.

Hammer was invited to join a group of Soviet advisors who were being sent to the Urals to report on conditions there. This trip changed his life forever. The refugees he saw on the three-day train trip to Ekaterinburg (now Sverdlovsk) were the characters in a nightmare he would never forget. "Cholera, typhus, and all the epidemics of childhood were rife among them," Hammer wrote. "I had imagined that my professional training as a physician had steeled me against human suffering, but the first vision of those refugees struck me cold with horror.

"During our twenty-four hours' stay in the station yard of Ekaterinburg, on our comparatively comfortable train, comparatively well-stocked with food, I received direct eyewitness knowledge of what a Russian famine meant. Children with their limbs shriveled to the size of sticks and their bellies horribly bloated by eating grass and herbs that they were unable to digest clustered around our windows begging piteously for bread—for life itself—in a dreadful, ceaseless whine. We could not help them. The busy stretcher-bearers carried the dead into one of the railway station waiting rooms, where they were stacked up in tiers . . . corpses, stripped naked because their clothes were too precious to waste, lay in heaps . . . the carrion crows and vagrant dogs fared well . . . to complete the tragic picture, there were grim tales of cannibalism, of mothers driven frantic, killing one child to keep the rest alive, and worse still, of butchers selling human flesh for profit."

But, as the train crawled through the Urals, Hammer saw vast stocks of minerals, platinum, semiprecious stones, and furs. When he asked the Russians why they did not sell the materials to buy grain, they answered that it would take too long to sell the goods and purchase food. "American grain was selling for under a dollar a bushel. So I asked the local officials, 'How much grain do you need to feed the whole population?' They said a million bushels. 'Well,' I said, 'I have a million dollars. I'll buy a million bushels of grain and send it over. And as each ship comes, you load it with something I can sell, to pay me.' It was 1921 and I was twenty-three years old."

The astonished and grateful Russians called a meeting of the Ural-Ekaterinburg Soviet and signed a contract immediately. A few days later, the official in charge of the train trip began receiving a message over the telegraph ticker directly from Lenin in Moscow.

"WHAT IS THIS WE HEAR ABOUT A YOUNG AMERICAN CHARTERING GRAIN SHIPS FOR THE RELIEF OF FAMINE IN THE URALS?"

Replied the official, "IT IS CORRECT."

Lenin: "DO YOU PERSONALLY APPROVE THIS?"

"YES," said the official, "I HIGHLY RECOMMEND IT."

"VERY GOOD," was Lenin's reply, "I SHALL INSTRUCT THE FOREIGN TRADE MONOPOLY DEPARTMENT TO CONFIRM THE TRANSACTION.

PLEASE RETURN TO MOSCOW IMMEDIATELY."

When Hammer returned to Moscow at the end of August 1921, he received a summons to report to Lenin's office at once. Passing through the Troitski Gate of the Kremlin, and scores of sentries, he was ushered into Lenin's office by Glasser, a small hunchbacked girl who was the leader's private secretary.

"Lenin rose from his desk and came to meet me at the door," Hammer wrote later. "He was smaller than I had expected, a stocky little man about five-feet-three, with a large dome-shaped head, wearing a dark gray sack suit, white soft collar, and black tie. His eyes twinkled with friendly warmth as he shook hands and led me to a seat beside his big flat desk. The room was full of books, magazines, and newspapers in half a dozen languages. They were everywhere, on shelves, on chairs, piled up in heaps on the desk itself, save for a clear space occupied by a battery of telephones. . . . During the hour or more our conversation lasted, I was completely absorbed by Lenin's personality."

As they talked in English, the Russian leader picked up a copy of the magazine *Scientific American*. "Look here," he said, running through the pages. "This is what your people have done. This is what progress means: building, inventions, machines, development of mechanical aids to human hands. Russia today is like your country was during the pioneer stage. We need the knowledge and spirit that has made America what she is today. . . .

"I heard you wanted to do medical relief work . . . it is good and greatly needed, but we have plenty of doctors. What we want here are American businessmen who can do things as you are doing. Your sending us ships with grain means saving the lives of men, women, and little children who would otherwise helplessly perish this winter. To the gratitude of these agonized people I add my humble thanks on behalf of my government. . . . What we really need are American capital and technical aid to get our wheels turning once more. Is it not so?

"The civil war slowed everything down and now we must start in afresh. The New Economic Policy (NEP) demands a fresh development of our economic possibilities. We hope to accelerate the process by a system of industrial and com-

Mamma Rose visits Hammer ("My son, the Asbestos King") at his mine in the Urals, 1923.

mercial concessions to foreigners. . . . Someone must break the ice. Why don't you be the first foreign concessionaire under our New Economic Policy."

Lenin and Hammer worked out plans for Hammer to take over an asbestos mine he had seen in the Urals. They sped up the bureaucrats, so that Hammer became the first American businessman to receive a commercial concession from the revolutionary government.

Hammer wrote his impressions of Lenin. "I somehow expected to meet a superman, a strange and terrible figure, aloof and distant from mankind. Instead, it was just the opposite. To talk with Lenin was like talking with a friend one knew and trusted, a friend who understood. His infectious smile and use of colloquial expressions, even slang, his sincerity and natural ways, put me completely at my ease. Lenin has been called ruthless and fanatical, cruel and cold. I refuse to believe it. It was his intense human sympathy, his warm personal magnetism, and utter lack of self-assertion or self-interest that made him great and enabled him successfully to hold together and produce the best from the strong and conflicting wills of his associates." Hammer saw Lenin once more, briefly, in the summer of 1922.

43

While passing through London, returning to Moscow from a trip to New York, Hammer noticed a bronze statuette in the window of the Leonard Partridge Antiques store on New Bond Street. He thought the statue, a monkey seated on a volume of Darwin's *Origin of Species*, holding a human skull in its hand, would make a nice gift for Lenin. Lenin was amused by the symbolism and remarked, "If instruments of destruction continue to grow, one day there will be only monkeys on earth." In view of the present dan-

ger of a nuclear holocaust, Lenin's prescience was remarkable.

With Lenin's blessing, Hammer began to prosper in the Soviet Union. Bureaucrats either became available to Hammer or he was able to bypass them. The Foreign Office moved him from the seediness of the Savoy Hotel to "The Sugar King's Palace," an opulent mansion across the river from the Kremlin. The palace had once belonged to a wealthy Ukrainian who had cornered the sugar market in czarist days. It is now

the British Embassy.

Besides the asbestos-mine concession (his mother, Rose, called him, "My son, the Asbestos King,"), Hammer organized the Allied American Corp. (Alamerico) and made a fifty-fifty joint venture with the Russian trade monopoly (Vneshtorg). He became the official representative in the U.S.S.R. for thirty-eight American companies, including Allis-Chalmers, Ford, U.S. Rubber, Underwood Typewriters, and Parker Pen. He bartered Russian furs, caviar, minerals, and lumber for the hard currency that was necessary to finance the operation.

Hammer married a beautiful Russian singer, Baroness Olga Von Root, fathered a son, Julian, and moved to another palatial mansion, known as "The Brown House." His brother Victor, who had majored in art at Princeton, came to Moscow and began helping him fill the new home with czarist art. "In Moscow," Armand says, "people didn't have money; they would bring their things into commission shops and put them

In the heart of the Urals, Hammer's asbestos miners pose for a portrait.

on sale for whatever they would bring. The government, hard up for cash, was doing the same thing, emptying some of the rooms of the Romanoff palaces to make quarters for government offices. There were very few buyers; mainly the embassies and Armand Hammer."

At that time, all pencils in Russia were imported. Since Lenin had announced that one of the goals of the Soviets was to teach each Russian to read and write, Hammer received permission to start a pencil factory, using technology and technicians that he wooed away from the Faber pencil cartel in Germany.

Within six months Hammer's pencil factory began turning out $2.5-million worth of pencils a year. By the next year the output was $4 million. The plant is still operating. In 1925, Hammer had five factories in Russia making pens, pencils, and other stationery.

Lenin died in 1924. But he had written to

Stalin about young Armand Hammer: "Fully support these persons and their enterprise, this is a small road to the American 'business' world and we must do everything to utilize this path."

When Stalin started to change Lenin's New Economic Policy, Hammer recognized that the writing was on the wall. In 1930, he took his wife and infant son and left Russia. "I couldn't do business with Stalin. Stalin didn't understand the importance of business," says Hammer.

"Lenin had died, and I had lost my friend. I sold out, and they let me take my personal belongings, including my art treasures, with me—my warehouses were full of all I had collected. From 1930 on, I had no international business. I did not return to Russia for thirty-one years."

After a short stay in Paris, where he dabbled as a private banker discounting Soviet notes for American companies selling machinery to the Russians, Hammer returned to New York at the

Hammer was exclusive agent for Ford and scores of American firms in post-revolutionary Russia. Here, in Rostov, February 1923, Hammer (over driver's shoulder) gives the Russians a first look at the Fordson tractor. He imported thousands. Young commissar Anastas Mikoyan, second from left (black coat, fur hat), looks on.

Hammer with his famous Black Angus purebred bull, Prince Eric, in 1953.

height of the Depression. His brothers Victor and Harry reported that there was very little market for the shiploads of czarist art that he had shipped to America. "Nonsense," said Hammer. "Not everybody could have gone broke in the Crash. It's just a question of proper marketing, and I think I have an idea."

He wrote letters to a dozen of the leading department stores in America, asking for an entire floor to display what he said were the greatest art treasures ever to leave Russia, and offering to share the profits of a huge sale. Only one store, Scruggs-Vandervoort in St. Louis, replied favorably. "COME IMMEDIATELY," they telegraphed. Loading their czarist art in dozens of trunks obtained from a bankrupt theatrical troupe, Armand and Victor embarked for the Midwest.

The sale was a remarkable success. With his innate talent for public relations, Hammer soon filled the St. Louis newspapers with photographs of his Romanoff treasures, which he closely asso-

ciated with the royal family, and stories of his adventures in mysterious Moscow. Hammer printed price tags that were embossed with the double-headed eagle crest of the Czars, below which was typewritten the history of each item.

On the opening day of the sale, with newspaper headlines proclaiming "Million Dollar Art Collection Goes on Exhibition and Sale Today," the police were called out to handle the lines of thousands of people waiting to enter the store. Before nightfall, Hammer called his brother Harry in New York to fill more trunks and bring the art to St. Louis.

The word soon spread through the mercantile establishment of America, and the prestigious Marshall Field department store in Chicago sent a vice president to St. Louis to persuade the Hammers to bring their exhibition to Chicago. The sale opened there three weeks later, with Dr. Hammer giving daily lectures on his adventures in obtaining the art in Russia. The exhibition was supposed to last three weeks; it continued for three years.

The Hammer Russian Art extravaganza traveled across the country. Stores, which paid for all advertising and salesmen's commissions, received a 40-percent discount on the art. The tour culminated in the greatest triumph of all, a three-year joint venture with Lord & Taylor in New York. Victor Hammer was dispatched to Russia to obtain more art.

When a Lord & Taylor vice president annoyed the Hammers by indicating that he knew more about czarist art than the brothers, they opened the Hammer Galleries on Fifth Avenue and 54th Street. By the height of the Depression, when America was preoccupied with unemployed apple sellers, soup kitchens, and breadlines, the Hammer Russian art sale had netted millions of dollars.

"I *told* you not everybody went broke," Hammer chided his brothers.

The Russian art triumph brought Hammer to the attention of the advisors of publisher William Randolph Hearst, possibly the most insatiable collector in American history. Hearst and his publishing empire had fallen on evil days, and the banks were closing in to collect $11 million as soon as possible.

Hearst's incredible art collection, which had cost him more than $50 million, was stashed in his three California estate homes, his castle, San Simeon, in California, his other castle, St. Donat's, in Wales, his Mexican ranchhouses, his hotel suites in New York—at the Ritz Towers, the Warwick, the Lombardy, and the Devon—and in warehouses in New York and Los Angeles. To save the publishing empire, Hearst's advisors prevailed upon him to sell at least half of the art collection. He agreed, but said that it had to be done with dignity and decorum.

The executives of the Hearst company retained Armand Hammer and the Hammer Galleries to handle the sale, for a 10-percent commission. Said Hammer at the time: "I think I have the greatest merchandising promotion any department store ever had—the sale of a $50-million art collection in a department store. Nothing like this has ever been attempted before."

The project went back and forth between New York's leading stores. Macy's missed the opportunity by refusing to let the Hammers set the retail prices. After much negotiation, the deal was set. Most of the collection would be sold through Gimbels, with a small boutique at Saks Fifth Avenue (which Gimbels also owned) handling certain choice pieces.

Hammer hired Hollywood set designers to create a setting for the great collection, Gimbels advertised for museum curators to work as salesmen, and Hammer invited 100,000 charge-account customers of Saks to the black-tie opening. Some 20,000 accepted.

The inventory was staggering: armor, arquebuses, war hammers, swords, tapestries, paintings, sculpture, stained glass, gold jewelry, furniture, gold and silver services, pottery, china, glassware, chandeliers, clothing, a Venetian frescoed council chamber from the sixteenth century, French *boiserie* paneling from

Hammer's mother visits with Eleanor Roosevelt at Campobello, which Hammer bought from the family and gave to the people of America and Canada as a peace memorial.

the fifteenth to eighteenth centuries, Gothic, Jacobean, and Georgian interiors, as well as a complete twelfth-century Cistercian monastery from Spain still packed in the 10,500 cases in which it was shipped to America.

At least 50,000 people toured the exhibition in the first week of the sale. The art critic of *The New York Times*, Edward Alden Jewell, wrote: "Only an experience-toughened specialist wearing blinders could, we cannot but decide, fail to be staggered by the sheer inclusive heterogeneity of this vast congeries of art objects of all periods and from all parts of the world. The impact is amazing."

On the first day, the Hammers sold more than $500,000 worth of art from the Hearst collection, and within a few months they had sold enough to pay off the Hearst bank loans. At that point Hearst canceled the sale and kept the rest of his collection.

Soon after the outbreak of World War II, and while the Soviets were allies of Hitler, Hammer exerted great efforts to help Great Britain. President Franklin D. Roosevelt assigned Hammer to work with Harry Hopkins to put together the fifty-destroyer Lend-Lease deal for Great Britain, which helped break the U-boat stranglehold and keep England in the conflict. Hammer was now in the barrel business, using white-oak staves imported from Russia. He went from barrels to bourbon, making blended bourbon from potatoes for the parched wartime market. He eventually bought the J. W. Dant distillery in Kentucky for a song, which he later sold to Schenley Distilleries for $6.5 million cash—after he had made J.W. Dant the number-one selling Kentucky bonded whiskey in America by pricing it the same as Seagram's Seven Crown with blended alcohol. Sales jumped from 70,000 cases to a million cases a year.

Hammer learned about thoroughbred breeding and artificial insemination while he was dickering to buy the world's prize Black Angus bull, Prince Eric, for whose offspring Hammer had a standing offer of $5,000 each. The recalcitrant owner was trying to overcharge him, asking an exorbitant price, even though the bull had stopped breeding. Hammer remembers when his long-time veterinarian, Dr. L. Mac Cropsey, showed him the bull's semen through a microscope: "There were thousands, thousands, and thousands of spermatozoa. All I could see were countless $5,000 bills swimming around." He bought Prince Eric for $100,000 and in the next three years, by artificial insemination, Prince Eric fathered more than a thousand calves and made a profit of $2 million for Hammer. Today, in Scottsbluff, Nebraska, Hammer's Occidental Petroleum Corporation maintains the largest Black Angus purebred herd in the world.

His marriage to the Russian baroness had ended amicably, and she had gone to Hollywood to resume her singing career. He then married Angela Zevely, a horsey New Jersey socialite who loved thoroughbreds, but, unfortunately, also strong drink. In the midst of the litigious divorce from his second wife and other family tribulations, Hammer received a letter from a lady friend he had met twenty years earlier, at the time of the famous Romanoff art sale at the Marshall Field department store.

Frances Tolman wrote from Westwood, California, where she had moved from Mundelem, Illinois, after her physician husband had died. She wrote that she had read of Hammer's troubles in, of all things, *The Police Gazette*, and asked if she could help him in any way. She gave her address, but not her phone number.

"You know Armand, he's very impatient," she says. "He couldn't get the phone number. The next thing I knew I looked out and he was walking up the driveway. We've been together ever since."

So Armand Hammer decided to retire in

Dr. Armand Hammer With best wishes, Lyndon B. Johnson

In the White House, Hammer chats with President Lyndon B. Johnson.

1956 and to live happily ever after.

However, as Hammer was lolling around Southern California, swimming and sunbathing and growing bored, a friend suggested at a cocktail party that as a possible tax shelter he should take a look at a small struggling oil company, Occidental Petroleum.

Hammer scanned the balance sheets, and though the 600,000 shares were listed at a value of slightly over $100,000, he deduced that the true value of the company was only around $34,000. Hammer thought it unwise to buy stock at eighteen cents a share, but the Hammers decided to loan the struggling company $50,000 for a 50-percent interest to drill two wells, figuring that if they were dry holes, the venture could be written off as a tax loss. Both wells hit.

The stock jumped to a dollar a share and Hammer began buying. When there was another chance for Occidental to buy a small field with nine producing wells from a cash-pressed wildcatter, Hammer went in with a New York real estate man for $1 million, with the same 50-percent interest.

The day after the agreement was signed, Hammer invited his attorney, Arthur Groman, to ride with him to Dominguez, California, to take

Hammer was sent on a presidential mission to Moscow in 1961 to meet with Russian leader Nikita S. Khrushchev.

a look at the nine wells. On the way, Hammer told the driver to stop at a drugstore. "I want to get a Polaroid camera," he said. When the attorney asked why, Hammer replied, "Because I've never seen a producing oil field up close in my life, and I want to get some snapshots to show Frances her oil wells."

Hammer worked out a stock deal with an old-time drilling contractor named Gene Reid, whose drilling rigs were already heavily mortgaged. "I've always wanted to be worth a million dollars, but after thirty years I've never made it," said Reid. "I have a feeling I'll make it with you." When Reid died in 1979, he was worth $30 million, all made on Occidental stock.

Hammer bought the Mutual Broadcasting System in the golden days of radio, signed Walter Winchell and Kate Smith, and sold it a year later for $1.3 million profit. By now, he was beginning to think of retirement.

Occidental was rolling by 1961. Near Lathrop, in California's Sacramento Valley, Occidental hit the second-biggest gas field in California, worth $200 million, where larger oil companies had hit dry holes.

Hammer found phosphate in northern Florida where none had been found before, combined that with sulfur he obtained when he purchased the Jefferson Lake Sulphur Company in Texas, and went into the fertilizer business.

In 1961, President Kennedy and Secretary of Commerce Luther Hodges sent Hammer on a trade mission to the Soviet Union. It was his first trip to the country since his departure in 1930. On the way home, he stopped off in Libya. "I saw what was happening in Libya," said Hammer, "and I wanted to get in on it."

Five years later, in the royal palace in Tobruk, King Idris said to Hammer, "Allah sent you to Libya." Occidental, drilling again where Mobil Oil had given up, had hit its first billion-barrel field. The company was already exporting more than 500,000 barrels of oil a day from the desert kingdom and was headed for a million barrels a day by 1970. Occidental Petroleum had become one of the largest international oil-producing companies in the world.

The King was overthrown and banished in September 1969 by Colonel Muammar al-Qaddafi. The years since have not been easy. Qaddafi's radical government threatened to confiscate the company's properties unless Occidental paid higher taxes and increased the price of oil. When Occidental capitulated, the rest of the major oil companies were forced to follow suit.

Says *Forbes* magazine: "In retrospect, Oxy's Libyan settlement may have been the most im-

A meeting with Russian leader Leonid I. Brezhnev in Moscow in 1973.

portant single event since the end of World War II—and one that marked a turning point for the modern world."

Hammer and Occidental hit again in the North Sea, where the output from its Piper, Claymore, and Scapa fields have exceeded 290,000 gross barrels a day over the past seven years. In 1984, the company announced still another billion-barrel strike, this time in the Caño Limon field in the jungles of Colombia, another area where major oil companies had tried and failed.

"Occidental, like Hammer himself, is something of an enigma," says *Forbes.* "Its growth record has been—astounding is the only word for it."

In May 1985, Hammer signed a letter of intent on behalf of Oxy with Royal Dutch Shell to sell one half of his Colombian discoveries for $1 billion. *The Wall Street Journal* called the Caño Limon strike in Colombia "Occidental's Black Gold Mine." *Forbes* said Caño Limon was "Armand's New Elephant," adding, "Neither age nor mounting criticism dims Armand Hammer's per-

petual optimism." In the interview, Hammer estimates that the Caño Limon discovery has doubled the $2.8-billion worth of Oxy.

Besides Occidental and the oil business, the chemicals business, the fertilizer business, the beef business, the plastics business, the Arabian horse business, and all the other facets of his operations, Hammer sits in the middle of a world of scurrying secretaries and vice presidents, takes and sends endless phone calls and telexes, flies all over the globe, pulls together art collections, endows cancer research and charities, and makes ceaseless efforts to bring world leaders together for one last chance at peace. There is incredible energy, awesome intelligence, and terrible toughness; also kindness, impatience, humor, and a prodigiously small taste for fools.

"I work fourteen hours a day, seven days a week. It keeps me young, it keeps me excited, it keeps my glands functioning," says the eighty-seven-year-old man of the eighties. "I never feel my age, especially when I am about to make a deal."

Los Angeles Times
Hopes Raised for PLO Pullout Soon
Details May Be Set Today, Lebanese Says, but Israeli Reaction Is Uncertain
A Tale of 2 Resorts: Growth Has Its Price
Suicide Attack by Armenians Kills 6 in Turkey

HOME: LOS ANGELES

The Hammers have three homes: the main residence in Los Angeles, the little house in New York's Greenwich Village, and the apartment in Moscow. It might be said, however, that the plane, *Oxy One,* is a fourth home, since the Hammers spend so much time in it: in 1984 they were away in the plane 105 days.

The Los Angeles home is an unpretentious two-story house in the university community of Westwood, only a few minutes from the Occidental offices. Hammer's two classic Rolls-Royces sit in the garage, but he commutes to the office in a chauffeur-driven Cadillac. Though the house is filled with fine art objects collected from all over the world and presented to Hammer by various heads of state, almost none of his fabulous $50-million art collection (five Rembrandts, four Rubenses, and works by Titian, Fragonard, Van Gogh, Cézanne, and Soutine) hangs in the house. "Just when I get used to a

At breakfast, Hammer has his coffee with the morning paper, beneath Monet's Rain.

A small plaque on his bedroom bookcase.

nice painting," sighs Mrs. Hammer, "he sends it off somewhere to another exhibition."

Indeed, many of the paintings in the house are copies that Mrs. Hammer, who is a skilled artist, renders in her upstairs studio. A striking Modigliani-style painting hanging over the stair-

case is a Frances Hammer copy that fools even art connoisseurs.

The house is filled with books, memorabilia, and telephones. When not traveling, the Doctor swims naked in his indoor pool for half an hour daily, does 500 stomach contractions, has a massage and a cold shower, then begins telephoning. "Sometimes I hear him at four in the morning, calling someone overseas," says Mrs. Hammer.

In his bedroom are four television sets—one immense console and three matched sets that President Lyndon Johnson used in his White House office to watch all three network news programs at the same time.

Wherever Hammer is—at home, in his limousine, in his offices, almost anywhere—he naps. "People always ask what is Armand's secret," says Mrs. Hammer. "Naps are his secret. He's like Winston Churchill. He can go to sleep anywhere for twenty minutes, and then come out ready to conquer the world."

55

Above. The Hammers dine in their Westwood home. Right. In their living room, the Hammers sit beneath Pissarro's Country Scene, surrounded by art treasures collected in their travels. They live very simply, with a small staff. Mrs. Hammer paints, takes care of the Doctor, attends to her investments, and packs bags for the next trip. The Hammers have lived in the Westwood house for twenty-nine years, since they were married in 1956. He was

divorced and she was a widow. Today, he is eighty-seven and she is eighty-three, and they fly more than 250,000 miles a year together. Says Mrs. Hammer, "I have a perpetual case of jet lag."

The Hammers with part of their
collection of Fabergé pieces from czarist
Russia and various pieces of Oriental
fine art.

Frances Barrett Hammer spent her early life in Illinois. Her first husband was also a doctor. When she is not traveling around the world with her husband, she paints in her studio at home, sometimes copying masterpieces from their collection, often doing paintings of friends like Princess Diana, above.

In his publication-filled bedroom, Dr. Hammer watches four television sets and reads the morning paper, while eating breakfast and arranging by phone to have tea with the visiting Deputy Prime Minister of Bulgaria.

A sampling of Hammer's awards, medals, trophies, certificates of commendation, decorations, and other honors, from every major country in the world.

Left. *Hammer phones from his study; his personal phone bill is reported to be half a million dollars a year. His staff reputedly can locate anyone on earth. One startled executive, vacationing on a radioless yacht in the Pacific, was summoned by a circling helicopter that dropped a bottle into the ocean with the message, "Call Dr. Hammer immediately."*

Right. *Every day when he is home, the Doctor swims in his indoor pool. A young woman once asked Hammer the secret of his longevity. He answered: "I don't smoke, I don't drink hard liquor (though I suppose I've manufactured more spirits than any man alive), I swim for half an hour every day, and I work very hard. I enjoy my work and it keeps me young." The woman said that her father did all these things and died at forty-nine. Replied Hammer, "He didn't do it long enough."*

As his chauffeur, Andy, follows with the bulging briefcase, Hammer starts for the office. He is frequently there for hours before the rest of the staff arrives, stays until early evening, and works most weekends.

THE CODEX GOES TO ITALY

A gasp went through the audience at Christie's London auction gallery on Friday, 12 December 1980. After eighty-five seconds of astronomical bidding, auctioneer Patrick Lindsay announced that the Leonardo da Vinci notebook known as the Leicester Codex had been sold to Dr. Armand Hammer for $5.8 million (including the auction fee), the highest price ever paid at auction for a manuscript.

Hammer, who had sat in the front row, making his bids with almost imperceptible nods of his head, said afterward, "I feel great. I'm very happy with the price. I expected to pay much more. I think it is the greatest acquisition I've ever made. I'm going to show it all over the world."

Earlier, British experts, focusing attention on the problem of losing national art treasures, had called the possible loss of the Codex a tragedy.

The sixteenth-century notebook contains seventy-two pages of hand-written notes and sketches by Leonardo, in reverse mirror-writing, exploring the color of the sky, how the moon is lit, canals, dams, the drainage of swamps, astronomy, cosmology, geology, the effect of tides and the principles of evaporation and condensation, bubbles, the theory of the siphon, snorkels, and the concepts of steam power and submarine warfare.

Since 1717 it had been the property of the Earls of Leicester, unavailable to the public. But now the manuscript had been put up for sale to satisfy British death duties on the estate. British authorities ordered a three-month delay in granting an export license while attempting to keep the 470-year-old Codex in England.

Hammer agreed to show the manuscript once a year in the United King-

En route to Italy, with members of the Occidental Board of Directors, Dr. Hammer sits next to the massive Codex container. Prior to the arrival of the Codex, Italian scholars and politicians had hinted that perhaps it should be left in Italy forever; later, when President Sandro Pertini presented Hammer with Italy's highest decoration, the Doctor promised that the Codex would go to Italy for exhibition every five years.

At Pisa airport, surrounded by soldiers, carabinieri, and plainclothesmen, Occidental security agents David Shields and Ed Birch bring the Codex container down from Oxy One as the welcoming Italians wait in armed anticipation.

Above. *Machine-pistol–toting guard at Pisa airport as the Codex is loaded for the trip to Florence.* Right. *The best-laid plans . . . the speeding convoy is halted at the toll station at the entrance to the autostrada, as security men scramble to forestall a possible ambush.*

dom and obtained permission from Prime Minister Margaret Thatcher to exhibit it in Washington's Corcoran Gallery in honor of President Reagan's inauguration. (Nancy Reagan cut the ribbon.)

Renamed the Codex Hammer by renowned Leonardo scholar Professor Carlo Pedretti of UCLA, the manuscript then went home to Italy for the first time in 265 years. Pedretti returned the Codex to its original form of eighteen sheets—four pages to a sheet—as it had been when Leonardo compiled it, and had the sheets mounted in Plexiglas modules so that

At a press conference in Florence's Museum of the History of Science, Dr. Hammer exhibits the specially designed display modules of the sheets from the Codex before they are put on exhibition at the Palazzo Vecchio.

all of the seventy-two pages could be seen and studied. Hammer brought the Codex back to Italy to be exhibited for three months in Florence's Palazzo Vecchio.

In a specially built, environmentally controlled container, designed to maintain constant humidity, the Codex was flown to Pisa, the nearest airport large enough to accommodate *Oxy One*. An army of security agents with machine guns and sawed-off shotguns guarded the arrival against the radical Red Brigades and thieves. With flashing lights and screaming sirens, the convoy took off for Florence.

The Codex was home again.

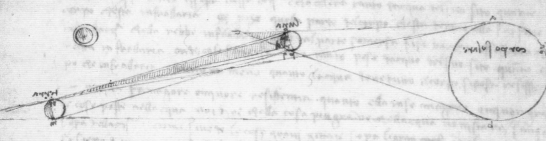

Two pages from the Codex Hammer.

*In Florence's Hall of the Five Hundred,
Hammer is welcomed by the leaders of the city.*

Above, top. *In the little village of Vinci, Leonardo's home town, some thirty miles from Florence, local officials install the Doctor as Honorary Citizen and Bearer of the Seal—which must be affixed to all laws—then show the Hammers the house where the great artist was born.*

Above, bottom. *In the local church, Hammer is shown the baptismal font of Leonardo and given a house for life, furnished and staffed with servants. The last recipient was Pope John XXIII. Right. The new honorary citizen of Vinci chats with a handful of other citizens on the main street of the village.*

MOVERS & SHAKERS

Above. *In Richard Nixon's New York office, Hammer meets with the former President.* Right. *French President François Mitterrand confers in his private office in L'Elysée Palace in Paris with Dr. Hammer and the interpreter.*

Presidents, premiers, prime ministers and popes, kings and queens, princes and princesses, sultans, emirs, generals and marshals and admirals, industrialists and publishers, media stars and Nobel Prize winners—Hammer moves among the leaders of the world like no other individual in history.

He visits them in their offices, palaces, country homes, and on their yachts and playing fields, exchanging views on politics, business, culture, science, and, frequently, on their favorite charities.

In one six-day, 18,000-mile jet slam in early 1985, Hammer had tea one afternoon with Prince Charles in London; the next day lunched with former Austrian Chancellor Bruno Kreisky in Mallorca, Spain, and dined that night with the King and Queen of Spain; the next evening he was in Rawalpindi, Pakistan, where President Zia presented him with the country's highest medal of honor at a state dinner at the palace; the next morning he jetted to Oman for tea with the Sultan, flew all the next day back to Washington for lunch and a State Department dinner honoring President Betancur of Colombia, and the same night flew home to Los Angeles.

Senator Paula Hawkins of Florida.

In Moscow, President Mika Spiljak of Yugoslavia.

With President Zia of Pakistan, in Beijing.

Poland's Premier Wojciech Jaruzelski, in the Kremlin.

India's late Prime Minister, Indira Gandhi, in Moscow.

With Soviet Ambassador Anatoliy Dobrynin in Washington.

At the United Nations, Secretary-General Pérez de Cuéllar.

Queen Beatrix of Holland.

Senator Jennings Randolph of Virginia.

President Sandro Pertini of Italy.

King Constantine of Greece.

First Lady Imelda Marcos of the Philippines.

First Secretary János Kádár of Hungary.

84

Party Chairman Hu Yao Bang greets the Hammers in Beijing.

Prime Minister Yitzhak Shamir of Israel.

Hammer's pal and lawyer, Louis Nizer.

Georgei Arbatov, Soviet expert on the United States and Canada.

Heavyweight clout: With Publisher Arthur O. "Punch" Sulzberger and Executive Editor Abe Rosenthal of The New York Times and America's leading gossip columnist, Liz Smith, of the New York Daily News.

85

Above. *Soviet Foreign Minister Gromyko
confers with Hammer in the Kremlin
after Andropov's funeral.*
Right. *In Beijing's Great Hall of the
People, Vice Chairman Deng Xiaoping
greets Hammer before a private meeting.*

Above. *In St. George's Hall in the Kremlin, at Chernenko's funeral, Hammer is greeted by Vice President George Bush and Secretary of State George Shultz.*

Left. *Hammer entertains former President Carter at a Los Angeles luncheon to raise funds for the Carter Library.*

Right. *Late-afternoon tea with Prime Minister Margaret Thatcher at 10 Downing Street. Afterward, Hammer left immediately for Heathrow Airport and flew back to Los Angeles to sleep at home the same night.*

THE ROYAL FAMILY

"Armand Hammer is a friend of princes and kings," said London's *The Sunday Times Magazine* recently. ". . . At the last count, he had given some $14,000,000 to charities which Prince Charles holds dear and had become a close personal friend of Britain's future king. Hammer feels that Prince Charles is a man of exceptional qualities who will take a vital role in the world to come. Prince Charles seems to have adopted Hammer as one of his favorite old men, especially since the death of his uncle, Lord Mountbatten."

In England, the Hammers have tea and dine at Buckingham Palace. In their living room in Los Angeles, in a place of honor on the piano, is a color photograph of Mrs. Hammer with baby Prince William on her lap.

For newborn Prince Harry, Dr. Hammer sent his father a Baby Jogger cart. Wrote the Prince, with thanks, "I can see that I shall have to get into extra training before venturing out with the youngest son."

Left, above. At a London dinner in Hammer's honor, Prince Charles toasted him, "To the man who conceived the North Sea Consortium and helped change the British economy."
Left. Host Hammer greets Prince Philip at a luncheon opening the 1984 Los Angeles Olympics. Right. In Beverly Hills, the Hammers escort Prince Andrew to a dinner they gave at the Beverly Wilshire Hotel to celebrate his visit to California.

At a gala dinner aboard Nelson's flagship, Victory, the Hammers dine with Prince Charles and Princess Diana to celebrate the successful raising of the Tudor warship, the Mary Rose. Dr. Hammer contributed mightily to the salvage fund.

RUSSIA

"Business is business, but Russia is romance," wrote young Hammer in an early autobiography in 1932.

It was a love affair he never got over. Ever since 1921, when the twenty-three-year-old medical school graduate from New York crossed the red-flagged border station at Sebesh by train from Riga, Latvia, Hammer has been fascinated and enthralled by Russia, its leaders, and its people.

Hammer lived in Moscow for nine years, flourishing in the Red capital as a capitalist businessman. He left during the Stalin era in 1930 and did not return for thirty-one years, when President John F. Kennedy and Secretary of Commerce Luther Hodges sent him in 1961 to help improve relations with Khrushchev after the U-2 incident.

Business rekindled the old romance, and by 1973 Hammer had concluded a $20-billion fertilizer transaction. In one year, he made twelve trips to the Soviet Union. He is one of the few private American citizens who can bring their own jets into the country, and the Soviet leaders have provided him with an apartment within walking distance of the Kremlin.

With all of his ties to Russia, including a physician father who helped found the American Communist Party, Hammer has never embraced communism. "I never bought it," he says. "When I talk to the Russians I always tell them that I am a capitalist, that I believe in capitalism, and that I don't believe their system works."

The Russia he sees today is vastly different from what greeted the young Doctor when he got off the train in the revolution-gutted city in 1921. "Moscow was utter desolation," he says. "The streets were almost deserted and great holes yawned in the roadway and sidewalks. The houses looked

Hammer could see the Kremlin and the Moscow River from the house where he lived in the twenties.

95

ready to fall to pieces, unpainted, many with patches of plaster falling away, and roofs half stripped of tiles. On many streets the walls and fronts of the houses were scarred by bullets of rifle- and machine-gun fire."

His life and work in Russia flourished after he obtained a million tons of grain for the starving people in the Urals, and he came to the attention of Lenin. "We don't need doctors. We need businessmen like you," said Lenin. "We are going to give concessions to foreigners; why don't you be the first?"

In the years that followed, Hammer lived in a palace overlooking the Kremlin, he held passbook Number One in the Soviet State Bank, he was the sole agent in Russia for scores of major American companies, he filled his house with Russian art, and he married a beautiful baroness.

Today, as one of the few living acquaintances of Lenin, he is a folk hero in Russia. His luggage is waved through customs at Sheremetyevo Airport, his Chaika limousine is ushered through police lines when the driver murmurs, "Doktor Hammer . . .," and in a hit play at the Moscow Art Theater, the young Hammer is depicted meeting with Lenin in the Kremlin.

"Business is business, but Russia is romance."

Left. The Doctor visits the place where he lived in the early days in Moscow, known then as "The Sugar King's Palace," after the rich man who owned it before the Revolution. Today it is the British Embassy.
Right, top. The head of the Russian State Bank, Vladimir S. Alkhimov, welcomes Hammer to his office with a Russian art book. Right. Walking down the stairs of the Pushkin Museum with the Mayor of Moscow, Vladimir F. Promyslov (right), after they cut the ribbon for the opening of the Moscow showing of the Codex Hammer.

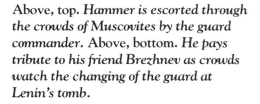

Above, top. *Hammer is escorted through the crowds of Muscovites by the guard commander. Above, bottom. He pays tribute to his friend Brezhnev as crowds watch the changing of the guard at Lenin's tomb.*

After attending the funeral of his friend Soviet leader Leonid Brezhnev, on 14 November 1982, Hammer returned to the grave behind the Lenin Mausoleum on Red Square to deliver a personal eulogy for the departed head of state.

Accompanied by American Senator Robert Dole and a few colleagues,

Hammer was greeted and escorted into the sealed area by the commanding officer of the guard.

Hammer remembered the funeral of Lenin. "This Mausoleum was built in two and a half days, with constant shifts of workmen toiling day and night . . . it was a period of intense cold, between thirty and forty below zero

Fahrenheit . . . in endless procession, day and night alike, the people of Moscow filed through . . . to pay their final tribute. Three quarters of a million men, women, and children formed that silent river, flowing through without a break . . . no king or emperor or pope ever received such final homage."

Hammer reads his hand-written eulogy for Brezhnev.

The Hammers are treated to a piano recital by one of the star pupils at a school for the children of workers at the pencil factory. Right. The Hammers receive the traditional Russian welcome offering of bread and salt.

This was a sentimental journey for the American tycoon. In the twenties, during his early days in Russia, an important commissar had told Hammer that a major government goal was to teach every Russian to read and write. Knowing that there was no pencil factory in the country, Hammer said he would like to obtain a license for the production of pencils.

Because there were no skilled technicians in Russia at that time, and the manufacturing techniques were secrets of foreign cartels, Hammer wooed pen-

The Doctor autographs a Russian-language copy of his autobiography for the director of the pencil factory.

cil experts from the big Faber plant in Nuremberg, Germany, to launch the project. The venture was a huge success and Hammer later sold the holdings to the Soviet government before he left Russia.

Now, half a century later, Hammer was invited to the school for the young children of the workers of his old plant, officially titled "The 647 Kindergarten and Crèche of the Moscow Writing Appliances Plant Sacco-Vanzetti."

Scrubbed and shining, the young students put on their recital after presenting the Hammers with the traditional Russian hospitality offering of bread and salt.

Afterward, the teachers and the current director of the factory entertained the visitors with tea and sweets. "To the director of the plant," Hammer inscribed in a Russian edition of his biography, "from the first owner."

As a teacher plays accompaniment on the piano, children do a dance beneath a large picture of Lenin, who some sixty years ago arranged for Hammer to create the pencil factory where their parents now work.

101

*Hammer is presented with a box of
pencils from his old factory.*

In the deepest heart of the Kremlin, Lenin's office is preserved exactly as it was on the day of his death; even the desk blotters are unchanged. Hammer met with the Russian leader here, and now he stands with his hand on the statue he presented to Lenin some sixty years earlier. The statue is a monkey sitting on a volume of Darwin contemplating a skull. Lenin remarked, "If instruments of destruction continue to grow, one day there will be only monkeys on earth."

Left. In a hit play about Lenin, This We
Will Win, at the Moscow Art Theater,
the young American, Armand Hammer,
is shown presenting a statue to Lenin in
the Kremlin office. Afterward, the real
Hammer and the stage Hammer meet
over the statue backstage (above), then
the directors of the theater serve drinks.

107

In another sentimental journey, Hammer visits the famous Moscow Circus and watches bareback acrobats gallop around the circle.

Left. Lobby of the Mezhdunarodnaja Hotel, part of Sovincentre, the world trade complex (top), which Hammer built for the Soviet government. The Russians call the complex "Hammer's house." Above. Hammer and producer Jerry Weintraub sign the guest book at Spaso House, home of the American ambassador. Right. In his heavily secured office at the American Embassy, Ambassador Arthur Hartman discusses Hammer's forthcoming meetings with the top Soviet leaders.

Amid funereal music and chandeliers swathed in black, in Moscow's Hall of Columns, where Lenin lay in state, Hammer pays homage at the bier of Soviet leader Yuri Andropov. Andropov's medals are displayed in front of the casket.

Red Square, 13 February 1984, the funeral of Andropov: Honor troops bring in the floral tributes as civilian cadres stand at attention with photographs of the deceased leader.

After standing for three hours in the bitter cold at the Andropov funeral, Dr. Hammer walks along the wall of the Kremlin, wearing the full-length mink coat he bought at Saks Fifth Avenue in Los Angeles specially for the occasion. "I remember the bitter cold at Lenin's funeral," he says.

After the funeral, in the czarist opulence of the Hall of St. George in the Kremlin, Hammer and visiting heads of state are ushered down a red carpet to meet the leaders of the Politburo.

Wearing on his lapel the Russian Order of Friendship of the People and the ribbon of a commander of the French Legion of Honor, Hammer is greeted by Soviet leader Konstantin Chernenko, who is wearing his soviet medals. The Russian observes that the American is the only person at Brezhnev's funeral who also stood in an honored place in Red Square on the day when Lenin was buried some sixty years before.

As the military band plays Chopin's
Funeral March, and the distant cannon
fire a final salute, the coffin of
Konstantin Chernenko is carried from
the caisson to the Lenin Mausoleum for
last rites.

In the Hall of St. George in the Kremlin, the new Soviet leader, Mikhail Gorbachev, greets Dr. Hammer and heads of state after Chernenko's funeral, 13 March 1985. Behind Gorbachev are Politburo members Tikhonov, Gromyko, and Kuznetsov.

HOME: MOSCOW

Above. *The Hammer's Moscow apartment is filled with Russian masterpieces, many of which Hammer brought from outside the Soviet Union. The Hammers have bequeathed them* to the Russian people. Some of the Russian masterpieces: Top, Children at the Piano, *by Bogdanova Belsky;* Above, At Her Bedside, *by Nicolas Kassatkin.*

Clockwise from left. *Hammer and Occidental colleague Don Cooper leave Hammer's Moscow apartment, passing the babushka who runs the building. More Russian masterpieces from the Hammer collection:* Le Tête à Tête, *by Vladimir Makovsky;* Constantin Makowsky's Boyarina at the Spinning Wheel; Woman with a Red Shawl, *by Philippe Maliavine;* Russian Hunters, *by S. Kolesnikoff.*

ARABIAN HORSES

Armand Hammer got his first Arabian horse from Lenin. "My first contact with an Arabian was in 1922; Mr. Lenin and General Budenny gave me a white Arabian stallion, which I had great fun racing. He won. I had him until I left Russia in 1930."

Fifty-one years later, Hammer went back to Russia and paid $1 million for another Arabian stallion, Pesniar. Though Hammer had been involved with raising purebred Angus cattle in the intervening years, horses had not been one of his major interests.

However, an acquaintance sought Hammer's Soviet expertise on the possibility of buying Pesniar. The Soviets had refused to sell, calling him the finest stallion in the Soviet Union. Hammer formed a partnership, flew to Pyatigorsk, and bought the horse.

It did not take Hammer long to realize the possibilities of the new venture. Oxy Arabians was in business.

The next year Hammer went to Poland and paid $1 million for El Paso, said to be the horse that money could not buy. Hammer convinced Polish leader Jaruzelski that the move would also help Polish-American relations.

In the four years since Oxy Arabians was formed, the Occidental subsidiary has spent $6.2 million building up the herd. Oxy Arabians now has 130 horses, whose value is estimated at more than $12 million.

Hammer sponsored the first big racing classic for Arabians, donating a $50,000 prize to the winner of the Hammer Cup.

Hammer, the art collector, is now a collector of horses. "They are art and beauty," he says, "alive and constantly changing."

Early morning, before the start of the prestigious Lasma auction in Scottsdale, Arizona, Hammer is surrounded by experts, making notes in his catalogue about which horses to buy. He bought sixteen mares for $3.25 million.

Clockwise, from bottom left. Show-business luminary Mike Nichols at the Lasma auction. Watching the horses being exhibited. Each winning bidder is presented with a bottle of champagne; Hammer got sixteen horses and sixteen bottles. Behind him is Texas merchant-prince Stanley Marcus. Hammer and the million-dollar horse, Pesniar. The Lasma auction is conducted with a Las Vegas flair, but the horses are the stars. Flanked by Lasma founder and Oxy Arabians consultant Dr. Eugene La Croix, Sr., Hammer bids with almost imperceptible nods. Alec Courtelis and John Connally are in the rear.

Arabian mare and foal being exhibited in Scottsdale before the auction. When Hammer bought his first Arabian, Soviet Life magazine said, "The American industrialist Armand Hammer did not repeat the Shakespearean phrase, 'My kingdom for a horse,' only because he did not have a kingdom. But he paid a million dollars at the traditional auction in Pyatigorsk in the northern Caucasus when he signed a contract to buy the thoroughbred six-year-old stallion, Pesniar."

Hammer checks out the mares and foals of the Oxy Arabians herd at their boarding farm. "I want horses that are as beautiful in action as they are standing still," says Hammer. "To get the best, you have to breed the best. Quality is the key to success."

As the horse on show is reflected in a mirror behind them, the Hammers, Merv Griffin, and Joan Irani, wife of Occidental President Ray Irani, look over the Oxy herd at the Lasma South boarding farm in Micanopy, Florida.

THE BEAUTIFUL PEOPLE

Left. At a twilight dinner in Los Angeles honoring Nobel laureate Dr. Linus Pauling, Hammer chats with Mrs. Cary Grant. Mrs. Hammer talks to Dr. Pauling and Dr. Carl Sagan, as Cary Grant talks across the table.

Apart from world leaders the Hammer experience encompasses a wide range of artists, writers, musicians, performers, scientists, and social and business leaders, ranging from Frank Sinatra to Dr. Evgeny Chazov, Kremlin physician to the Politburo.

There are luncheons, yacht trips, charity galas, and endless dinners. As Hammer skips across the continents on Oxy One, the tuxedo and tails are always packed.

At a cocktail party in Beijing, the Doctor holds hands with Jacqueline Kennedy Onassis.

141

Aboard Malcolm Forbes's yacht,
Highlander, Dr. Hammer sits between
Barbara Walters and the host at the start
of Forbes's annual Fourth of July cruise
around Manhattan to view the fireworks.

Clockwise, from left. *Architectural Digest Editor Paige Rense beams at a party at the Hotel Bel Air in Los Angeles as Dr. Hammer embraces his old friend Baron Hans Heinrich Thyssen-Bornemisza. Media czar John Kluge and his wife, Patricia, chat with Mrs. Hammer. "Dear Abby," Abigail Van Buren (left), with Dr. Hammer and Occidental board member Rosemary Tomich. At a charity concert at the Universal Amphitheater in Los Angeles, the Doctor talks with host Frank Sinatra. Aboard Malcolm Forbes's yacht, Barbara Walters and economist Alan Greenspan ask Hammer for information about the Soviet Union.*

13 March 1982: After visiting the Piper offshore drilling rig on the North Sea, Hammer visits his friend, Stanton Avery, the American label manufacturer, at Avery's castle, Dunbeath (right), on the Scottish coast. Above, top. The host welcomes Hammer when the helicopter lands. Above. The ladies greet their husbands at the door to the castle.

At Dr. Hammer's eighty-sixth birthday celebration in Beverly Hills, he is flanked by his good friend, the noted Russian cellist, Slava Rostropovich, and King Constantine of Greece. Rostropovich, who had soloed with a chamber orchestra for the festivities, embraced his pal "Armanchik," poured several vodkas, and closed the salutation with a kiss.

In refutation of the old maxim, "Money can't buy happiness," four of the richest men in the world try to grin and bear it at a party at the Hotel Bel Air in Los Angeles. Arab entrepreneur Adnan Khashoggi, Dr. Armand Hammer, MGM owner Kirk Kerkorian, and the host, Baron Thyssen-Bornemisza, put on a brave front.

GOOD WORKS

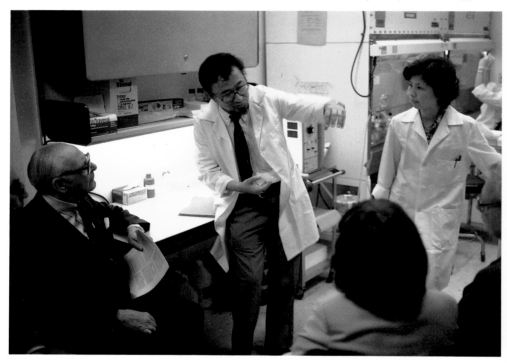

With other members of the President's Cancer Panel, Dr. Hammer visits a research team at UCLA and is briefed by Dr. Paul Terasaki of the UCLA Tissue-Typing Laboratory.

At eighty-seven, Armand Hammer is a man who has everything and has done everything. But beyond the enormous thrust of his business activities, Hammer is constantly immersed in a world of charitable contributions and hard work for causes he believes in.

Many of his donations are anonymous, others are better known. They cover a wide gamut of interests: science, medicine, art, exploration, archaeology, human rights, education, and other areas that move him.

Sometimes the output is enormous. In March 1985, Hammer gave $1 million to UCLA to create a center for research and study on Leonardo da Vinci. Less than six weeks later, in New York, he donated another $1 million for the renovation of the Arms and Armor Gallery of The Metropolitan Museum of Art. A week later, on the day of a party celebrating his eighty-seventh birthday, Hammer made a gift of $500,000 to his friend Slava Rostropovich's National Symphony Orchestra as part of its endowment.

Hammer summed up his philosophy in a speech he gave in 1984 at the National Press Club in Washington, D.C.: "I've been a man of many dreams and I've been fortunate to see many of them come true. But my greatest dream remains to be fulfilled—a lasting peace and a cure for that most dread of diseases, cancer."

Hammer inspects a tissue sample under a microscope. "Cancer is a scourge that we must get rid of," says Hammer. "I remember the terrible despair my father felt when he had to try to treat people suffering from polio, for which there was then no known prevention. I'm sure we can beat cancer just as we've beaten polio, thanks to Jonas Salk."

Cancer Research

Above, top. *In Washington, Hammer discusses cancer research with President Reagan's chief scientific advisor, Dr. George A. Keyworth. Above, bottom. In 1977, Hammer donated $5 million to Columbia University, where he and his father went to medical school, for the establishment of the Julius and Armand Hammer Health Sciences Center.*

In 1981 Dr. Hammer announced that he would award $1 million to the scientist who found a cure for cancer within the decade, and that another million would be given in yearly grants of $100,000 to others who make significant contributions to cancer research.

He has also donated $5 million each to Columbia University's Julius and Armand Hammer Health Sciences Center and the Salk Institute for cancer work. Each year he funds the Armand Hammer Cancer Conference at the Salk Institute, where scientists from all over the world gather to share their work and knowledge.

In 1984, President Reagan appointed Hammer to a second term as Chairman of the President's Cancer Panel, which advises the President on the status of cancer research in America.

With Dr. Jonas Salk at the
Salk Institute for Biological Studies
in La Jolla, California.

United World College

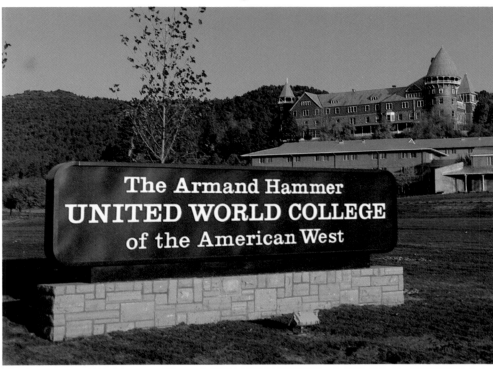

The concept of the United World Colleges was developed in Great Britain, under the leadership of Lord Louis Mountbatten. His nephew, Prince Charles, took over as President of the movement in 1979, and he interested Dr. Hammer in establishing an American branch to supplement the schools already functioning in Wales, Canada, Singapore, Italy, and Swaziland.

The United World Colleges seek better world understanding by bringing together young students from many countries. The young people live and learn in close proximity, in a way that would be impossible if they attended schools in their own homelands.

Students aged sixteen to nineteen, selected through tough competition in their own communities, attend the colleges for two years. Upon graduation, they are eligible to enter the second year at American colleges or the first

While the Armand Hammer United World College is under construction, Dr. Hammer tours the grounds with his friend and lawyer, Arthur Groman, Dr. Theodore Lockwood, President of the college, and former aide James Pugash.

year at institutions abroad.

Dr. Hammer paid $1 million for a property in Montezuma, New Mexico, which is topped by an old Victorian resort hotel. The Armand Hammer Foundation then spent $5.5 million to build classrooms, administration buildings, dormitories, a library, a gymnasium, and the other facilities that are necessary to operate a modern college. Contributions to date have totaled about $15 million.

The school opened in October 1982, and Prince Charles and Dr. Hammer were present for the dedication.

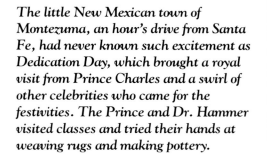

The little New Mexican town of Montezuma, an hour's drive from Santa Fe, had never known such excitement as Dedication Day, which brought a royal visit from Prince Charles and a swirl of other celebrities who came for the festivities. The Prince and Dr. Hammer visited classes and tried their hands at weaving rugs and making pottery.

159

In a sea of students dancing in their native costumes, Prince Charles joins a conga line on Dedication Day.

The first Graduation Day, 24 May 1984.

For graduation at the Armand Hammer
United World College, the Beach Boys
give a concert, courtesy of Hammer's
friend, theatrical impresario Jerry
Weintraub. The exuberant students
dance all over the New Mexican
countryside.

Wells Cathedral

Wells Cathedral is like a great jewel that dominates the green English countryside of Somerset. Construction began in 1176 under Bishop Reginald de Bohun, and over the next three centuries the careful builders followed the Bishop's plans to create a building that is faithful to the unity of his artistic vision.

Today the venerable edifice is feeling its age, and there is a great need of stone replacement and preservation. Carvings of nearly 300 medieval figures, including knights and angels, are deteriorating, due to weathering over the past 750 years and to some vandalism in the seventeenth century.

Prince Charles, who is very interested in the preservation of the beloved national monument and is now President of Wells Cathedral, enlisted the aid of Dr. Hammer. The Hammers flew to Wells, toured the cathedral, talked with the Dean, architects, conservators, lunched with the local gentry, and prepared to make a sizeable contribution to the preservation of the old church.

Dr. Hammer surveys the preservation work on Wells Cathedral, with the Very Reverend Patrick Mitchell, Dean of Wells.

The Human Rights Conference

In 1979, following the deaths of René Cassin and Eleanor Roosevelt, Hammer felt there was a gap in the world human rights dialogue.

He created the Armand Hammer Peace and Human Rights Conference, bringing together more than a hundred international leaders. The first meeting was held in Oslo six years ago, and has been followed by annual meetings in Campobello; Warsaw; Aix-en-Provence, France; Hyde Park, New York; and Madrid.

At the Hyde Park meeting, the leaders gathered at the grave of Franklin D. Roosevelt, as former French Premier Edgar Fauré and others shielded themselves from the noon sun. With the late President's son, James Roosevelt, Hammer discussed the old Roosevelt vacation home, Campobello, which Hammer purchased and gave to the people of the United States and Canada in 1961 as an international peace park.

An Orphanage in Colombia

In Bogotá, Colombia, which has one of the largest populations of street children in the world, the Hammers donate one million pesos to an orphanage that brings the children back to the land by teaching them farming.

At the Fundacion Granjas Infantiles del Padre Lona, which operates five farms for 200 orphans, Dr. Hammer presents the check to the director, Father Jaime Preito, as Occidental's Colombia chief, Edward Quinones, and his wife, who help sponsor the work, look on.

Transglobe Expedition & The Raising of the Mary Rose

Above. *Thousands of cheering onlookers and an armada of festooned boats line the Thames on 29 August 1982 to welcome the Transglobe Expedition back to Greenwich, where it had set out three years earlier.* **Right.** *Aboard the* **Benjamin Bowring,** *flagship of the* **Transglobe Expedition,** *Prince Charles and Dr. Hammer welcome back the twenty-nine circumnavigators.*

"It is splendidly mad," said Prince Charles when he heard of an expedition proposed by Sir Ranulph Twisleton-Wykeham-Fiennes, an ex-British Army officer. Ran Fiennes spent seven years planning the Transglobe Expedition. His dream was to circumnavigate the globe the hard way, 38,500 miles over both poles, across four continents, three oceans, and ten seas, under conditions of extreme cold and heat. Prince Charles became expedition patron, and the mad explorers scrounged money, equipment, and supplies. Among the major contributors was Dr. Hammer, who also backed a major film on the feat. A feat it was. The expedition came back three years later, a huge success. Prince Charles and Hammer greeted the expedition members in Greenwich, as the Prince hailed their "courage, endurance, will power, and sheer bloody-mindedness."

On 19 July 1545, a horrified King Henry VIII of England watched as the four-masted warship *Mary Rose*, with nearly 700 men on board, capsized while repelling an attack of the French armada. The wreck moldered for 437 years in the chilly waters of the Solent, off Portsmouth.

Then beginning in the mid-1960s, a dedicated team of historians and marine archaeologists took on the task of locating and salvaging the *Mary Rose*. Once the wreck was exposed, it was a race against time to protect the boat and its contents from final destruction due to devastating tides, marine organisms, and accidental damage. In nearly 25,000 dives between 1979 and 1982, experts and amateurs recovered the *Mary Rose*'s hull and 17,000 objects. The artifacts recovered include a wealth of Tudor memorabilia: bronze cannons, boxes of clothing, medicine chests, carpenters' tools, coins, arrows, pocket sundials, and even bones of drowned men. This massive treasure trove presents the best picture to date of English naval power and life at sea in the Tudor period.

The Twenty-First Prince of Wales became interested, made ten dives to inspect the ship in its cold, muddy resting place, and became president of the *Mary Rose* Trust, a charity dedicated to saving the wreck. He enlisted the aid of his friend, Dr. Hammer, who became President of the Board of Directors of the American Society for the Archaeological Study of the *Mary Rose*.

Hammer contributed more than $500,000 to the most expensive underwater archaeological salvage operation in history. On 11 October 1982, the remains of the *Mary Rose* were lifted from the water in a specially molded 560-ton lifting frame and cradle, hoisted by a floating crane.

Said Alexander McKee, the historian-scuba diver who located the watery grave of the *Mary Rose* sixteen years earlier, "This is a dream come true."

Portsmouth, England, 10 November 1982: Admiral Sir James Eberle shows the Hammers the newly raised Mary Rose, still in its salvage cradle. It has since been ensconced in a permanent naval museum.

A HUNT
IN HUNGARY

Telki, one of the great hunting preserves of the world, is a few miles outside of Budapest. A royal remnant of the old Austro-Hungarian Empire that has survived a century of social change, the preserve has been maintained by the present government of Hungary as a hospitality center for important visitors. The great stone hunting lodge, the coterie of loden-clad guides, and the endless forests filled with deer, wild boar, and other game are a Valhalla for serious sharpshooters, from archdukes to first secretaries.

In the fall of 1984, knowing that Dr. Hammer would be in Budapest on business, the Hungarian leaders invited him to a shoot, and Hammer included his friend, hunting buff Otis Chandler, Chairman of the Board and Editor-in-Chief of Times Mirror. Chandler has pursued big game in the Himalayas, on the tundra and the veldt, and throughout most of the rest of the hunting world.

Hammer was already famous at the preserve from a previous hunt, when he got five animals in one day with four shots, including a record wild boar and two deer that he killed with one bullet. This time, though the group hunted from before dawn, Hammer never got a shot. But Chandler scored with a red stag and a mouflon sheep.

Left. Dr. Racz Antal, director of the Telki hunting preserve in Hungary, adjusts Hammer's telescopic sight. Soviet leader Brezhnev was a famous guest at the lodge. Above. Hammer is outfitted with the proper hunting hat.

175

Before sunup, Hammer stalks the game with his Hungarian guide.

Meanwhile, back at the lodge, after a hard morning in the wilderness, Otis Chandler displays his red stag as an attendant serves the traditional pear brandy to the famished hunters.

Above. *Gypsy violinists serenade Hammer at the Kalocsa restaurant in the Hilton Hotel in Budapest.* Right. *Hammer introduces Chandler to his friend János Kádár, First Secretary of the Hungarian Socialist Workers Party.*

WASHINGTON ELITE

Because Washington is the power center of America, Hammer commutes between the capital and Occidental's Los Angeles headquarters, sometimes two or three times weekly.

From his office on Pennsylvania Avenue, Hammer confers with government leaders, sees visiting heads of state or their ambassadors, attends cocktail parties and state dinners, and appears before Congressional committees. In the national capital he is a familiar figure.

Frequently Hammer leaves Los Angeles in the early morning, flies to Washington for an important dinner, leaves directly for the airport, and boards *Oxy One* for Los Angeles. With the difference in time zones, he often makes it home by midnight.

Above, top. **Hammer is greeted by the President of Austria, Rudolf Kirchschläger, and Vice President George Bush at an Austrian reception. Above. With House Leader Tip O'Neill at a Capitol party, and with former**

Attorney General William French Smith. Right. With the Reagans and O'Neills at a Ford Theater première that Hammer hosted. On 2 June 1985, Dr. Hammer made a $500,000 endowment to the historic theater.

13 March 1982: Just off the plane from Moscow, at the Austrian Embassy in Washington, Hammer chats with New York Times *editor James "Scotty" Reston and his wife.*

Above, top. Host Hammer with Russian Ambassador Dobrynin and visiting Politburo member Vladimir Vasil'yevich Shcherbitsky, at a Washington dinner and hockey game that Occidental gave for the Russian delegation.
Above. Hammer is awarded the Knight Commander's Cross by the Austrian Foreign Minister, Willibald Pahr, at the embassy in Washington.

Right. In Occidental's Washington office on Pennsylvania Avenue, the Doctor confers with members of his staff: Executive Assistant Rick Jacobs (left); Washington chief Bill McSweeny, President of Occidental International (middle); and Communications Vice President Frank Ashley (right).

After a hard day in the halls of government, the Hammer party takes a stroll through the cherry blossoms at the Jefferson Memorial.

AN EMPIRE OF ART

"Armand Hammer is a fantastic human being, one of the most interesting and delightful men I have known. When he was young, he was a hero to the starving peasants in the Urals. In old age, he has become a hero to the covetous museum directors in the United States. His early life was spent converting rubles into dollars. His later life has been spent converting the profits which accrued into a collection every American museum would like to have."
—John Walker, Director Emeritus, National Gallery of Art, Washington, D.C.

"I've always liked to collect. I used to collect stamps," says Hammer, "but pictures are something more than just collecting. You are connecting yourself with something that really is immortal, something that has survived all these centuries. You are preserving something for posterity . . . paintings connect you with history."

Hammer and his younger brother Victor, began collecting czarist art in Russia in the twenties and they have never stopped. Today, the Doctor owns a controlling interest in the Hammer and Knoedler galleries in New York, as well as one of the world's most important private art collections.

He gave one collection of Old Masters to the University of Southern California in 1965, and began a new accumulation of art. Today, the Armand Hammer Collection is a remarkable assemblage of more than 100 American and European masterpieces that span five centuries. Hammer has collected paintings and drawings by French Impressionists, Post-Impressionists, and Old Masters, but he has also gathered works by Picasso, Chagall, and other modern masters, as well as by Americans from Remington to Wyeth.

In 1976, Hammer began still an-

Dr. Hammer in the Knoedler Gallery in New York.

190

other collection when he purchased more than 4,000 lithographs by Honoré Daumier and added to them original oil paintings, drawings, and sculptures by Daumier. He acquired Leonardo daVinci's Codex Hammer in 1980, paying $5.8 million, the highest price ever recorded for a manuscript.

The paintings and drawings do not hang in his home for his personal perusal. Instead, they constantly tour the world and have been exhibited in Tokyo, Moscow, Stockholm, Paris, Caracas, Madrid, Mexico City, Edinburgh, Beijing, Jerusalem, and twenty-three cities in the United States.

The Hammers have bequeathed their drawings to the National Gallery of Art in Washington, D.C., and the paintings, the Daumier Collection, and the Codex to the Los Angeles County Museum of Art, where they will be housed in the Frances and Armand Hammer Wing. The Doctor has been a benefactor of the Corcoran Gallery in Washington, to which he has made many donations, and he has been named a Lifetime Trustee of the Gallery. He has contributed greatly to the restoration of the Jacquemart-André

Above. *The Hammer brothers, Armand and Victor, at the Hammer Galleries in New York. "The Russians gave me a big house to live in, but there were no furnishings," says Hammer, "so I sent for my brother, Victor, who had studied art at Princeton, to come over and help me furnish my house. Victor went out and found he could buy works of art and antiques in commission stores for the price of ordinary furnishings . . . our house became a museum, filled with paintings, French furniture, eighteenth-century furniture . . . Aubusson tapestries, rugs, Sèvres china, beautiful silver, for all of which Victor paid a fraction of their value. And that's how I became interested in art."*

192

Museum in Paris; for this gesture, the Museum's name was expanded to include the words "Armand Hammer." He has also made donations to the Louvre, for which he received the Cross of the French Legion of Honor.

The love of art and of exposing great beauty to as many people as possible is mixed with his joy in the chase. "It's fun. It's a hunt. I get a certain joy out of finding rare works," he says. "The works of human genius speak across the ages to our senses and our hearts. Sharing these wonderful creations is reward enough for any man."

Above. *Dr. Hammer inspects restoration on a Degas with renowned conservationist David Bull, who is now with the National Gallery of Art in Washington.*
Left. *After donating $1 million to New York's Metropolitan Museum arms and armor department, Hammer remarked, "I wanted to do something for my home town."*

The Frances and Armand Hammer
Wing of the Los Angeles County
Museum of Art is the home of the
Hammer collection and the Codex when
they are not traveling around the world.
Right. *Two Californians in shorts view a
painting by John Singer Sargent, Dr.
Pozzi at Home.*

The Codex Hammer and other masterpieces on exhibition in Los Angeles. On a recent visit to the museum, Mrs. Hammer was approached by a security guard who asked, "You're Mrs. Hammer? Did your husband really paint all these pictures?"

197

Above, top. *The Mayor of Moscow,*
Vladimir F. Promyslov, inspects the
Codex Hammer at the Pushkin Museum
on opening night. Above. *In Lima's*
Museum of Fine Art, Peruvian
President Fernando Belaunde Terry
attends the opening of the Daumier
show. Right. *At Beijing's China National*
Art Museum, Dr. Hammer and the Vice
Minister of Culture, Mr. Si Tu Hui
Ming, cut the ribbon to open the show.
This was the first time since the
Revolution that Western art from a
collection had been exhibited in China.

In December 1984, the Codex Hammer went on exhibit in Madrid's Prado museum. Queen Sofia attended the opening. Pursued by European and American television teams, the Doctor toured the museum, making the obligatory stop to view both versions of the Maja.

Left. *In Moscow's Pushkin Museum,
beneath a huge copy of Michelangelo's
David, Hammer holds a press conference
for the opening of the Codex Hammer
exhibit.* Right. *Following a gala at
Washington's National Gallery of Art, in
honor of President Reagan's second
inauguration, the Hammers depart with
Director J. Carter Brown.*

HOME: NEW YORK

In 1919, when the young Armand Hammer was a medical student in New York, he bought a small coach house in Greenwich Village and converted it into a home. Later, he bought the house next door and knocked down the adjoining wall. Today, though he could easily own the finest mansion or penthouse on Park Avenue, the cozy little house filled with sentimental memorabilia is still Hammer's New York home.

There is a stuffed sailfish trophy on the balcony of the high-ceilinged living room, a Gauguin copy by Mrs. Hammer in one corner, and an ancient adding machine that must have figured in the growth of Occidental on the cluttered desk. In the dining room there is a fireplace made of jade from one of Hammer's mines, and a set of czarist china that Hammer brought out of Russia decades ago stocked on shelves along one wall.

The house still has the feeling of a college boy's pad, from long ago.

An old adding machine sits on the desk in his little house in New York's Greenwich Village. New and old volumes fill the bookcase.

The living room of the Hammer house in Greenwich Village. The painting over the fireplace, Sir Thomas Lawrence's The Best Children, *formerly belonged to the Metropolitan Museum of Art.*

Above. *A painting,* Paysage, *by Maurice Vlaminck, is lit by an antique lamp from the Paris Metro.*
Right. *Viebert's painting,* The Startled Confession, *surrounded by art books and artifacts.*

Dr. Hammer and his Washington chief, Bill McSweeny, give TV anchor Phyllis George Brown a tour of the New York house during an interview for CBS Morning News. Hammer brought the collection of Romanoff china in the dining room out of Russia in the thirties. Years later, at a dinner that Khrushchev hosted in the Kremlin, the Hammers were served on the same china.

OCCIDENTAL PETROLEUM

As Chairman and Chief Executive Officer of Occidental Petroleum, the eighty-seven-year-old Hammer is field marshal of a $15-billion-a-year money machine. Occidental, America's ninth-largest oil company, is a bustling behemoth of 41,000 employees that embraces oil, gas, coal, chemicals, fertilizers, beef, Arabian horses, and a score of other interests, with ties in every part of the world.

Hammer ricochets across the globe overseeing Occidental operations, leaving behind him a trail of exhausted executives wondering how the steel-trap brain can remember so many details. One day he is wearing a hard hat in Pakistan, checking a new oil strike; the next night he is in Washington in black tie attending a State Department dinner for the President of Colombia, where a recent Occidental oil discovery in the jungle augurs a radical improvement in that country's economy.

With operations in thirty-four states in America and thirty-seven countries, including Abu Dhabi, Argentina, Australia, Belgium, Bolivia, Brazil, China, Colombia, Ecuador, Egypt, Ireland, Japan, Madagascar, Mexico, the Netherlands, Oman, Pakistan, Peru, the Philippines, Singapore, the Soviet Union, Tunisia, Venezuela, and the United Kingdom, the old field marshal has to keep moving.

North Sea Oil

Hammer, with his friends John Paul Getty and Lord Roy Thomson, established the North Sea Consortium, the largest single operation in that area. Over the past seven years, the operation has produced 290,000 gross barrels of oil a day. When Hammer and Thomson were hammering out the deal in London, they set off for lunch in the latter's Rolls-Royce and in the restaurant discovered that neither of them had enough cash-in-pocket to pay the bill.

Left. Occidental Petroleum Corporation 1985 Board of Directors, left to right: Morrie A. Moss, Louis Nizer, Paul C. Hebner, William J. McGill, Zoltan Merszei, Arthur B. Krim, George O. Nolley, Aziz D. Syriani, Rosemary Tomich, John W. Kluge, Armand Hammer, Arthur Groman, C. Erwin Piper, Ray R. Irani, Robert L. Peterson, Albert Gore. Right. Shrouded in the North Sea spray, Occidental's Piper Drilling Platform pumps away. Dr. Hammer, in a red hard hat, surveys the work.

Perched above the waves of the North Sea, the Piper drilling platform functions in an area that experiences some of the worst weather in the world. Waves peak at 100 feet and higher, and winds howl above 100 miles an hour. The crews work twelve-hour shifts for seven days, then have a week ashore.

An hour from Aberdeen, Hammer's helicopter circles the Piper platform before landing for an inspection and lunch. Working under difficult conditions, the crews are provided the best of food. Each week they consume more than 160 pounds of butter, 700 pounds of flour, 1,000 pounds of fruit, 560 gallons of milk, 2,000 pounds of meat, and 1,000 pounds of vegetables. No women or liquor are allowed on board.

Oil Strike in Colombia

In 1984, on a parcel of land deep in the Colombian jungle, where Exxon and British Petroleum had previously drilled dry holes and departed, Occidental's oil experts found a mammoth, billion-barrel oil field that will transform the economy of that country. A pipeline system is now being built to transport the oil over the Andes to an export terminal at the Caribbean port of Coveñas.

In September 1984, Hammer flew to Cartagena, Colombia, where he stayed in the presidential villa and conferred with his executives. He then journeyed on to Bogotá, where he joined President Belisario Betancur to sign the joint-venture pipeline agreement between Occidental and Colombia.

He also began making arrangements with the Colombian President to bring the famous Hammer collection of paintings by Honoré Daumier to Bogotá for exhibition.

At the presidential holiday villa in Cartagena, Occidental drilling and exploration chief, Dave Martin, points to the discovery sites as he briefs Hammer on the billion-barrel strike. Colombia's Minister of Public Works, Dr. Rodolfo Segovia Salas (in the blue shirt), and, next to him, Occidental President Dr. Ray Irani, listen intently as Oxy's Colombian chief, Ed Quinones, and Latin American head, Jim Taylor, spell out the details of the biggest oil strike in Colombian history.

Bogotá, 10 September 1984: Surrounded by aides and executives, President Betancur and Dr. Hammer stride through the presidential palace to sign the pipeline agreement on the big strike.

Ecuador

Left. In January 1985, Hammer flew to Guayaquil, Ecuador, to sign an agreement with President León Febres-Cordero giving Occidental exploration rights to a large block of land in the country's eastern jungle region. The agreement was Ecuador's first step in fifteen years to attract foreign investment to search for oil, a fundamental factor for the economic recovery of the country. "This is an oily basin, and our block is favorably located," said Hammer. "We expect to be successful."

Venezuela

Right. In the presidential palace in Caracas, beneath a painting of Simón Bolívar, President Jaime Lusinchi speaks through his interpreter with Dr. Hammer, Occidental General Counsel Gerald Stern, and American Ambassador to Venezuela George Landau.

Early Oil Days

In the oil fields of the San Joaquin Valley of California, where Hammer made his first big strike, the pumping units never stop.

Big Cattle

At Ankony Shadow Isle Ranch, outside of Scottsbluff, Nebraska, Occidental runs the largest herd of purebred Black Angus cattle in the world—4,128 head in the spring of 1985.

Big Coal

Dwarfed by a mountain of coal at the new Baltimore export terminal, Island Creek Coal executive Stonie Barker Jr., Hammer, Charles Gillmore, President of the Curtis Bay Terminal, and former U.S. Senator Albert Gore inaugurate the facilities on opening day.

Colorado Shale Oil

According to government sources, there are 1.8 trillion barrels of oil locked in the oil shale rock of Colorado, Utah, and Wyoming, more than twice the world's known oil reserves, and enough to make America independent of other sources for more than a hundred years.

The techniques of recovery·are still costly. Occidental in ten years has spent more than $160 million of its own funds on its research program at Logan Wash, Colorado.

Hammer arrives by helicopter to check the site, smells the oil deep in a Rockies cave, runs a diesel truck on the condensed light shale oil, and samples a cake baked in honor of the 300,000 barrels produced thus far.

224

CHINA

The sleeping giant of China began to stir four years ago under the prodding of Chairman Mao's successor, Deng Xiaoping. When Deng visited the United States in 1979, he was introduced to Dr. Hammer at a Houston rodeo.

"You don't have to introduce Dr. Hammer," said the Chinese leader. "We all know you in China. You're the man who went to Russia in 1921 to help Lenin when Russia was in trouble. Now you've got to come to China."

Hammer began commuting to Beijing. Because of the possibilities of offshore oil drilling and access to China's huge coal reserves, Western executives were pouring into the Chinese capital. Deng invited Hammer to fly his private jet into China and to stay with his team as guests of the government at the Diao-Yu-Tai State Guesthouse.

Doing business in China entails endless meetings with ministers, vice ministers, chairmen, and vice presidents, coupled with luncheons and dinners given by the hosts and reciprocated by the foreign guest Sample menu: Mongolian hot pot, abalone in egg white, vegetarian's goose with sauce, fried vegetarian's prawns, three balls with cabbage, and compote of lotus seeds.

There are also side trips to the Great Wall and the Ming tombs, but business occupies the bulk of Hammer's time. For Occidental Petroleum, this business has resulted in offshore drilling in the South China Sea and an agreement to start digging the world's largest open-pit coal mine, in Shansi Province.

The Pingshuo mine in Shansi, 220 miles from Beijing, sits on a bed of wide-ranging bituminous coal reserves estimated at 1.4 billion tons. The $600-million project is a joint venture between the Chinese government and Occidental. It is the largest Sino-American joint venture in history.

But dealing with a generation of Chinese officials who were taught all their lives to distrust foreign capitalists requires much negotiation and many trips to Beijing by Hammer. "You've got to learn a lot of patience."

Top. **In the Great Hall of the People, Hammer presents Vice Chairman Deng Xiaoping with a specially commissioned painting of his native village.** *Above.* **After a meeting in the heavily guarded** compound of the Central Committee, Hammer and Premier Zhao Ziyang emerge from Zi-Guanq-Ge, the Pavilion of Purple Light, famous for many historic conferences.

On 29 April 1984, in the Great Hall, Hammer and the Chinese officials sign the project agreement for the world's largest open-pit coal mine in Pingshuo, Shansi Province.

After the coal-mine signing, Hammer is interviewed by the world press.

At a dinner given by Occidental Petroleum in the Great Hall's main dining room—possibly the largest room in the world—host Armand Hammer

Above, top. *After an Occidental dinner at the Beijing Hotel, government officials and the Hammers mingle with the local entertainers.* Above, bottom. *Ronald Reagan slept here. The Chinese hosts show the Hammers the Presidential Bedroom in the villa that Reagan occupied at the Diao-Yu-Tai state guest house. The villa was rebuilt for Reagan's visit; the Hammers occupied the same suite on a subsequent visit to China in May 1985.*
Above. *A meeting with the Minister of Agriculture, Lin Hujia. Sometimes there are five or six meetings a day at different ministries.*

Above. At the International Friendship Forestry Garden outside Beijing, the Hammers take part in a tree-planting ceremony. Left. The Hammer tree, with its tag. Right. A visit to a famous temple, Da-Chun-Si, Temple of the Big Bells.

DR. ARMAND HAMMER APRIL 28, '84

The grounds of the Diao-Yu-Tai government guest house in Beijing, where visiting heads of state—and Dr. Hammer—stay.

Most major Chinese government ministries have their own cultural troupes that tour the country. On an evening in Beijing, the Song and Dance Ensemble of the Ministry of Coal Industry of China put on an opera, *The Silk Road Episode, for the Hammer delegation.*

After the opera, Hammer was escorted on stage by the coal ministry officials to meet the cast. Said the English-language program notes: "The hosts and guests said goodbye to one another at the Parting Pavilion. The traditional friendship between the people of China and other countries would flourish forever."

Left. At Da-Chun-Si, Temple of the Big Bells, there is a museum of ancient Chinese bells; the Hammers are escorted inside the largest bell to see the inscriptions.

Right. China has a law against the export of giant pandas. After long and fruitless negotiations, American officials of the 1984 Los Angeles Olympic Games appealed to Hammer to see if he could prevail upon the Chinese to loan two pandas to Los Angeles as a symbol of the People's Republic. Hammer spoke to Vice Chairman Deng Xiaoping, who changed the law, and a few weeks later the two pandas, with a large delegation of attendants, were flown to Los Angeles as Occidental's contribution to the Olympics. Hammer met them at the airport and escorted them to the Los Angeles Zoo, where they were installed in a specially built air-conditioned pavilion.

THE WORLD
IN A WEEK

Los Angeles, California; 9:00 A.M., Wednesday, 27 March 1985. *Oxy One* sweeps down the runway at LAX and makes the turn toward Houston. In his office/cabin, the Doctor finishes the morning newspapers he started in the limousine to the airport and begins to go through the papers in his massive briefcase. He has already attended an early-morning (6:45 A.M.) Drexel Burnham breakfast for 1,000 institu-tional investors, where he spoke briefly and received an ovation. He calls in his staffers to get ready for a 2:00 P.M. shale oil meeting with Jim Ketelsen, CEO of Tenneco, at the Houston Airport, en route to London.

London, England; 10:00 A.M., Thurs-day, 28 March. In his usual suite at Claridge's Hotel, Hammer's business meetings start. At 4:30 P.M. Hammer

American flags whipping in the wind, the Hammer convoy drives from the Oman airport into the desert capital, Muscat.

has tea with Prince Charles at Kensing-ton Palace. The Prince is suffering from a cold, and Doctor Hammer gives him some of his favorite anti-flu pills. Take-off for Spain is set for early the next morning.

245

In his office aboard Oxy One, Hammer confers with aides Rick Jacobs, Executive Assistant, and Frank Ashley, Vice President for Communications.

Over coffee and dessert, after lunch, Hammer chats with his friend Bruno Kreisky, former Chancellor of Austria.

The Hammers have dinner with King Juan Carlos and Queen Sofia, and their daughter, Infanta Doña Cristina, in the Palacio de Marivent, before departing for Pakistan.

Palma de Mallorca, Spain; 1:30 P.M., Friday, 29 March. At the yacht club, the Hammers have lunch with their good friends: former Chancellor of Austria Bruno Kreisky, Mrs. Kreisky, American Consular Agent Bartolome Bestard, and Mrs. Bestard. That evening the Hammers have dinner with King Juan Carlos and Queen Sofia at the Palacio de Marivent. They reboard *Oxy One* that night and depart for Pakistan.

Islamabad, Pakistan; 11:00 A.M., Saturday, 30 March. At the airport welcome, Hammer advises his drilling experts that he wants to visit Occidental's oil strike at Dhurnal, three hours away—though he is scheduled for dinner with President Zia that evening. With a motorcycle escort, the convoy rushes to the oil field in the Punjab. Hammer inspects the wells and returns to the city in time for dinner. At the Presidential Palace, Zia presents Hammer with the nation's most important decoration for foreigners, the Halal-i-Quaid-i-Azam, and hosts a state dinner in honor of the Doctor.

Above. *In his private residence, before dinner, President Mohammed Zia ul-Haq and Foreign Minister Sahabzada Yaqub Khan, congratulate Dr. Hammer on his newest decoration.*
Left. *With Occidental exploration chief Dave Martin, Dr. Hammer inspects the company's newest oil strike in that country.*

Muscat, Oman; 11:30 A.M., Sunday, 31 March. The Occidental party is greeted at the airport by Dr. Omar Al-Zawawi, Special Adviser to the Sultan. With American flags flying on the cars, Dr. Zawawi escorts the Hammers and their entourage to his seaside mansion, where they will spend the night. After lunch, Dr. Zawawi takes the Doctor and the American Ambassador to Oman, John Countryman, to the

Left. *The Hammers are greeted at the airport by Dr. Omar Al-Zawawi, Special Adviser to the Sultan.*
Below. *In a special pavilion on his estate, Dr. Zawawi gives a dinner party for the American guests.*

Royal Palace for a meeting with the Sultan, His Majesty Qaboos bin Said, and the Minister of Petroleum and Minerals, Said Ahmed Al-Shanfari; in the twilight meeting at the Sultan's seaside pavilion, the four men sip tea and discuss business. Occidental receives important new oil concessions. That night, Dr. Zawawi entertains at his home with a lavish dinner party attended by Dr. Zawawi's brother, Qais Abdul Munem Al-Zawawi, the Deputy Prime Minister.

Right. *Waiting to see the Sultan. Oman's Minister of Petroleum and Minerals, Said Ahmed Al-Shanfari, confers with Dr. Zawawi; Dr. Hammer in background.*

Muscat, Oman; 10:00 A.M., Monday, 1 April. After breakfast at the American Embassy, *Oxy One* takes off for the United States.

Washington, D.C.; 4 P.M., Monday, 1 April. Twenty-three hours after taking off from Muscat, Oman, *Oxy One* lands at Dulles Airport; the Doctor goes right to his office and to work.

Washington, D.C.; 12:30 P.M., Tuesday, 2 April. Dr. Hammer has lunch with President Belisario Betancur at the Colombian Embassy residence. That night, he attends a State Department dinner in honor of President Betancur hosted by Secretary George Shultz. After dinner, the Hammers go directly to Dulles Airport and board *Oxy One*.

Los Angeles, California; 11:30 P.M., Tuesday, 2 April. *Oxy One* lands at Los Angeles Airport, having flown 18,000 miles in six days. Hammer's chauffeur and bodyguard, Andy, is waiting with the mail. The Hammers go home.

Above, top. Dr. Hammer and Dr. Zawawi have coffee from a golden pot in the guest quarters of the Zawawi estate.
Above. Dr. Hammer and the American Ambassador confer with the Sultan, Dr. Zawawi, and Minister Shanfari.
Right. Dr. Hammer catches a few winks as he waits on the Palace grounds to meet the Sultan.

254

At the flight engineer's post on Oxy One, Dr. Hammer makes another phone call.